Business Guides on the Go

"Business Guides on the Go" presents cutting-edge insights from practice on particular topics within the fields of business, management, and finance. Written by practitioners and experts in a concise and accessible form the series provides professionals with a general understanding and a first practical approach to latest developments in business strategy, leadership, operations, HR management, innovation and technology management, marketing or digitalization. Students of business administration or management will also benefit from these practical guides for their future occupation/careers.

These Guides suit the needs of today's fast reader.

L. Martin van der Mandele
Henk W. Volberda
Rob B. Wagenaar

The New Professional Service Firm

How Consultants, Accountants, and Lawyers Need to Reinvent Themselves

L. Martin van der Mandele
Leiden, The Netherlands

Rob B. Wagenaar
Wagenaar and Associés BV
Bunde, The Netherlands

Henk W. Volberda
Amsterdam Business School
University of Amsterdam
Amsterdam, The Netherlands

ISSN 2731-4758 ISSN 2731-4766 (electronic)
Business Guides on the Go
ISBN 978-3-031-06133-2 ISBN 978-3-031-06134-9 (eBook)
https://doi.org/10.1007/978-3-031-06134-9

© The Editor(s) (if applicable) and The Author(s), under exclusive licence to Springer Nature Switzerland AG 2022
Translated and updated from the Dutch-language edition: "De nieuwe professional service firm" by L. Martin van der Mandele et al., © The Authors 2019. Published by Scriptum. All Rights Reserved.
This work is subject to copyright. All rights are solely and exclusively licensed by the Publisher, whether the whole or part of the material is concerned, specifically the rights of reprinting, reuse of illustrations, recitation, broadcasting, reproduction on microfilms or in any other physical way, and transmission or information storage and retrieval, electronic adaptation, computer software, or by similar or dissimilar methodology now known or hereafter developed.
The use of general descriptive names, registered names, trademarks, service marks, etc. in this publication does not imply, even in the absence of a specific statement, that such names are exempt from the relevant protective laws and regulations and therefore free for general use.
The publisher, the authors, and the editors are safe to assume that the advice and information in this book are believed to be true and accurate at the date of publication. Neither the publisher nor the authors or the editors give a warranty, expressed or implied, with respect to the material contained herein or for any errors or omissions that may have been made. The publisher remains neutral with regard to jurisdictional claims in published maps and institutional affiliations.

Illustrations by Joris Mensink

This Springer imprint is published by the registered company Springer Nature Switzerland AG.
The registered company address is: Gewerbestrasse 11, 6330 Cham, Switzerland

Contents

1	**Disruption Is On the Way**	1
1.1	We Cannot Go On Like This	1
	1.1.1 Accountants Diversify as Auditing Declines	3
	1.1.2 Lawyers Automate as They Specialize	5
	1.1.3 Consultants Threaten to Lose Focus	9
1.2	The Four Major Disruptions of Our Professional Existence	14
	1.2.1 Technology Disrupts	14
	1.2.2 New Generations: A Different Breed of Professional	18
	1.2.3 What Do the New Generations Want?	19
	1.2.4 Critical Clients Find New Solutions	24
	1.2.5 Surviving Complexity	25
1.3	Current Strategies Will Not Help	30
	References	31
2	**Understanding How Professionals Work: Building Blocks for the Future**	35
2.1	Understanding Our Business Model	35
2.2	Services: What We Deliver	36
	2.2.1 External Perspective	37
	2.2.2 Creativity	39

    2.2.3 Leadership: Ad Interim 39
    2.2.4 Connections and Network 40
    2.2.5 Coach and Trusted Advice 41
2.3 Three Ways to Deliver Professional Work 41
2.4 Compensation: How Professionals Are Paid 43
2.5 What Is Our Business Model? 45
2.6 How We Work Today: Our Archetypes and Their Limitations 47
    2.6.1 Our Gentlemen's Club 47
    2.6.2 The Professional Corporation 50
    2.6.3 The Flexfirm 53
2.7 Today's Archetypes Are Not Sustainable 55
    2.7.1 Which Model Is the Most Forward-Looking? 57
References 61

3 Profiting from Disruption 65
3.1 Introducing Case Studies on Business Communities 65
3.2 Two Expert Communities: Cambridge Technology and Merlin 66
3.3 Flexible Consulting and Law: Eden McCallum and the Montage Legal Group 68
    3.3.1 Flexible Job: With Quality Results! 71
3.4 Computer-Based Professional Services: Rocket Lawyer 73
3.5 A Community of Software Firms: BSO/Bureau for Software Development 75
3.6 The Berkeley Research Group: A Professional Community with a Wide Range of Services 77
    3.6.1 A Unique Business Model 78
    3.6.2 A Quick Start 80
    3.6.3 Challenges 81
3.7 What We Have Learned from These Cases: Conclusions 81
References 83

4	**The Professional Service Community: The Way Forward**	**85**
	4.1 What the Professional Service Community Looks like and how it Works	85
	4.1.1 From Firm to Community	85
	4.2 The Community Has a Future, unlike the Old Archetypes	89
	4.3 Vision, Leadership, and the Pop-Up Team	90
	4.3.1 What Should the Leadership of our Community Look like?	90
	4.3.2 Coordination of Accounts and the Pop-up Project	91
	4.4 Sources of Professional Value: Brainpower, Skills, and Knowledge	92
	4.4.1 Finding and Retaining Brainpower in our Community	92
	4.4.2 Skills and Capabilities	93
	4.4.3 How Do we Acquire New Skills?	95
	4.4.4 Knowledge in our Community	95
	4.5 Creating Professional Value through Organization, Good Economics, and the Right Culture	98
	4.5.1 Organizing our Community	98
	4.5.2 How Should we Govern our Community?	98
	4.6 Creating the "Superculture" in the Community	99
	4.6.1 How Do we Build our "Superculture"?	100
	4.7 How to Make Money with our Community	102
	4.7.1 Work Steps to Arrive at the Appropriate Economic Model	104
	4.8 Reputation as the Sustainable Foundation of our Community	104
	4.8.1 Reputation Is the Name of the Game	104
	4.8.2 Reputation: A Special Challenge for our Community	106
	4.9 Delivering Value with our Community	108
	4.9.1 Which Services we Want to Deliver with our Community	108
	4.10 A Promising List of Clients	109
References		**114**

5   Foundations of the Successful Professional Community   117
- 5.1   Our Professional Community Needs Strong Foundations   117
- 5.2   What Does Success Mean in a Community?   118
- 5.3   Connectivity, Compatibility, and Commonality   118
  - 5.3.1   Connectivity   118
  - 5.3.2   Compatibility   120
  - 5.3.3   Commonality   122
  - 5.3.4   Conclusion   123
- 5.4   The Successful Community Professional   123
  - 5.4.1   What Characteristics Should we Expect Them to Have?   124
- 5.5   Trust, Tolerance, and Transparency: Cornerstones of Culture   126
  - 5.5.1   Trust   126
  - 5.5.2   Tolerance   130
  - 5.5.3   Transparency   132
- 5.6   Growth: The Great Imperative   134
- 5.7   Synergy: Translating Strong Foundations into Measurable Success   136
- 5.8   Innovation and Renewal   137
  - 5.8.1   Why Innovate?   137
  - 5.8.2   Alienation and Spin-Offs Threaten   140
  - 5.8.3   How Do we Strengthen Innovation and Keep Innovative Teams on Board?   140
  - 5.8.4   How Do we Start and Manage Innovation?   141
- References   142

6   Fieldwork: Monday Morning Actions   145
- 6.1   Off to Work!   145
- 6.2   Understand Our Current Strategic Position and Disruptions   146
  - 6.2.1   Step 1: Follows Chapter 1 of This Book   146
- 6.3   Evaluate Our Business Model   147
  - 6.3.1   Step 2: Follows Chapters 2 and 3 of This Book   147

6.4	Assemble Our Community Model		148
	6.4.1	Step 3: Follows Chapter 4 of This Book	148
	6.4.2	Agree on a Vision for the Community and Its Core Consequences: Reputation, Brand, Standards	149
	6.4.3	Decide on the Leadership of Our Community and Its Pop-Up Projects	149
	6.4.4	Define Our Sources of Professional Value: Brainpower, Competences, Knowledge	149
	6.4.5	Determine Our Organization, Economics, Culture, Strategy	150
6.5	Invite Partners to Our Professional Community		151
	6.5.1	Make Sure the Foundations of Our Professional Service Community Are in Place: Step 4: Following Chapter 5 of This Book	151
	6.5.2	Get Our Colleagues On board	152
6.6	Make Sure We Remain on Track		154

Closing Remarks   155

Afterthoughts   157

Index   159

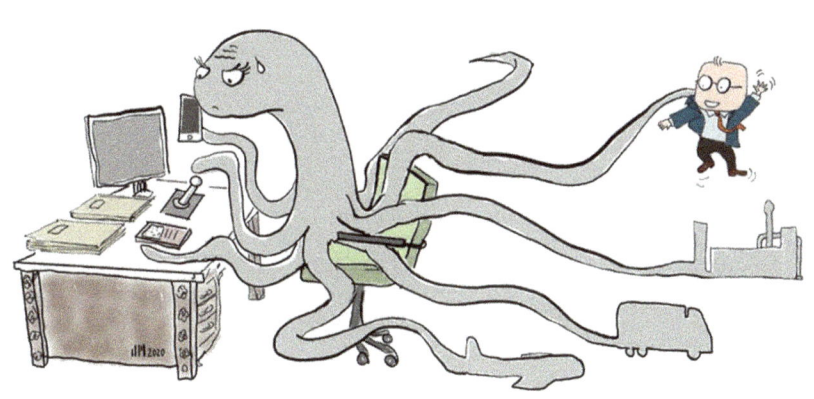

Welcome to the New Professional Service Firm

You are—or will be—the leader of a professional firm. Or you manage an advertising agency or an engineering or architectural firm. Or a research institute. You have an ambition to lead your firm. You may be the frustrated client pictured on the facing page. Maybe you are simply interested in the dynamics of a fascinating business.

You have noticed some of the changes going on in professional firms. Technology taking over, new ways of working. New competitors—small, innovative firms with new ideas and enthusiastic people. Large established firms with lots of money to throw at interesting proposals and clients. Clients who are more and more willing to shop around for expertise and who appoint in-house staff to deal with the routine work.

You feel that your current way of working will no longer lead to long-term success. Increasingly, your firm can no longer deliver all the expertise that your clients demand. And you no longer attract the best and the brightest.

You are aware of the substantial resistance to change in your organization. Life has been good in recent years and the firm in its current form can be expected to last until the end of many partners' careers.

Where do you want to end up? As a small, subcritical workshop where thinking is dominated by three worries: where do we find the next bright staff member? Where do we get the next engagement? And how can we deliver the expertise that the client wants for the price that he or she

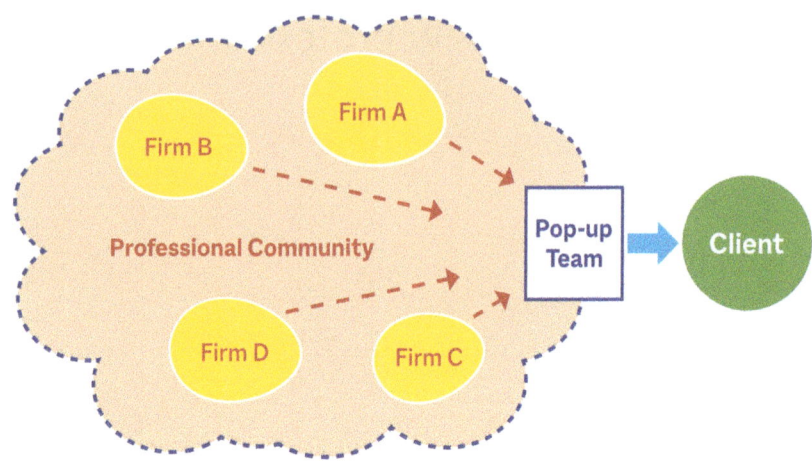

Fig. 1 The professional community

expects? Or do you want to finish as part of a large and powerful corporate machine, with clients complaining about the costs, your colleagues complaining about the bureaucracy, and juniors complaining and leaving.

The following pages provide an answer to the challenges described above. The professional community is a synergistic team of organizations that share a vision on their role in society as well as key values such as ethics, quality, and client care (see Fig. 1). They are also independent in designing their own business models—recruitment, training, knowledge management, structures, processes, and earnings formula.

As you start to make a move you and your partners must understand how the world has changed and has left your firm behind. You must have a vision of the road ahead for your business.

And you must understand what the tools are that you can apply to make the necessary changes. This book will help you on your way.

This book is divided into six chapters:

- **Chapter 1** summarizes some of the important trends in our environment and helps us understand the disruptions that will fundamentally threaten our firm—sooner or later.
- **Chapter 2** describes the business model of a professional firm, which is quite different from the well-known models of industrial or service

companies. It also describes the archetypes that dominate our business today. We now have the building blocks to enable us to construct our own model out of the many options available.

- In **Chapter 3**, we test a number of case descriptions of firms that are successfully developing in the direction of a professional community: our proposal is, after all, simply a new combination of proven organizational approaches.
- In **Chapter 4**, we propose and describe the professional community, which is a good—and for many firms the best—response to the challenges that we see today. This is neither the old gentlemen's firm nor a large professional corporation or a non-committal flexfirm, but an enterprising form in between.

> *We have a lot of illustrations that comment on our writing and hopefully inspire you. In our drawings we meet our professional and his diverse colleagues, as well as their client whose many activities keep all her arms busy.*

- In **Chapter 5**, we systematically discuss foundations such as trust, growth, and professionalism and how they can be developed. Our professional community can only be successful with these foundations.
- **Chapter 6** lays out the path ahead, from Monday morning onward.

We wish you enjoyment, enlightenment, and inspiration from reading these chapters[1]. And, above all, success in implementing these ideas in your professional community!

Martin, Henk, and Rob

---

[1] To maintain a modicum of readability in this book the term "his" is used instead of the more correct "his/her." With apologies, "his" should be read as being gender-neutral.

About the Authors

Martin van der Mandele is board member of a number of knowledge institutes. His career spanned more than 40 years as President of RAND Europe, European Management Team member of Arthur D. Little, and strategy consultant in the USA and across Europe with Booz Allen & Hamilton.

Henk Volberda is Professor of Strategy & Innovation at Amsterdam Business School of the University of Amsterdam and Director of the Amsterdam Centre for Business Innovation. Volberda holds various executive and advisory positions. He is member of the supervisory board of NXP Semiconductors Netherlands and Apollo Tyres Europe and member of the scientific advisory committee of the Netherlands Defence Academy. In addition, he is expert member of the World Economic Forum and Fellow of the European Academy of Management.

Rob Wagenaar is management consultant and leadership mentor. After a career with KPMG and De Galan & Voigt, he was founder of two consulting firms, WagenaarHoes and ASI Consulting. He had a number of supervisory positions in the profession, including the presidency of Ooa (Dutch Society of Management Consultants) and vice-presidency of the International Council of Management Consulting Institutes.

List of Figures

Fig. 1.1	Worldwide revenues of "big four" accounting firms	5
Fig. 1.2	Decrease in law offices in the USA	6
Fig. 1.3	Increasing differentiation in law firms	6
Fig. 2.1	Delivering value in professional services	36
Fig. 2.2	What we deliver	37
Fig. 2.3	Mode: how we deliver	42
Fig. 2.4	How we are paid in professional services	43
Fig. 2.5	Risk and return of different professional service contracts	45
Fig. 2.6	A business model for the professional service firm	47
Fig. 2.7	Disruption of our business	56
Fig. 2.8	Exploration and exploitation by archetypes	59
Fig. 3.1	Size and scope of professional communities	66
Fig. 3.2	Comparison of BRG with selected consultants	79
Fig. 3.3	BRG revenue growth 2010–2017	80
Fig. 4.1	The professional community	89
Fig. 4.2	Sourcing knowledge	97
Fig. 4.3	Choosing the right contract form	103
Fig. 4.4	Interesting clients	111
Fig. 5.1	Synergy potential of communities	137

Between three rocks and a hard place... I love to be challenged...

1

Disruption Is On the Way

1.1 We Cannot Go On Like This

Our business has been flourishing. Most consulting, accounting, and law firms have enjoyed wonderful growth and great profitability in recent years. But most of our services are vulnerable to changes in society and business. And the COVID-19 pandemic was a clear sign that our future is more uncertain than ever. It is clear that the earnings and operating models for professional services—such as those of our firm—will undergo fundamental change in the coming years.[1] This change is being enabled and triggered by new and increasingly powerful IT systems that have a profound impact on professional work itself—like artificial intelligence for advisors, block chain for audit work, and big data in the legal profession. A further important driver of change, in particular in the Western world, are the job demands of bright new generations that have great talent but also different career aspirations. Yet another important impetus are our sophisticated clients who do not shy away from introducing innovative forms of insourcing and outsourcing and from trying out new contractual arrangements. We face competition not only from well-known players but also increasingly from new innovators and large expanding services corporations. At the same time, contracting in professional

---

[1] Christensen and Overdorf (2000).

services is shifting from traditional hourly fees to fixed fees, risk participation, and even equity participation. But "no more than 10% of the market has any idea of the disruptions that we face," to quote the managing partner of a global accountancy firm.

We see our trusted and successful firms with their experienced partners, who used to make decent margins with the help—and leverage—of a large group of hardworking juniors, coming under pressure. At the same time, professional services corporations are growing and extending their scope, both geographically and functionally. The management costs of these companies are increasing accordingly and they are forced to put up their rates, while many clients have the feeling that their larger suppliers no longer add value. Multinational firms have a function, as long as international expertise and connections are called for. Medium-sized companies, however, fall between two chairs and are in danger of sinking and disappearing. Their scale does not provide the benefits of the really large providers, but they do have a cost base that makes competition with specialized small suppliers difficult. Many have merged or simply disappeared in recent years, such as Booz & Co (now PWC) and Braxton in consulting, Debevoise & Plimpton in law, and Arthur Andersen in accounting.

If we want our professional firm to still be a success five to ten years from now, we must act immediately. When we go through an economic downturn, we see the radical changes that take place around us accelerate and become life-threatening.[2] Traditional solutions to provide cost savings, a new software package, and an alliance are useful but do not suffice. Carrying on in the same way will ultimately be fatal. But precisely because business has been so good in the past, we hesitate, thinking "things might go wrong, but it will probably be after my time." This may hold true for older partners, but certainly not for the firm as a whole. Fortunately, we have a business model available that does meet the new requirements of clients and professionals, and that is made possible by the new information and communication technologies: *the professional community*.

Let us take a closer look at the three professions that are the core of our analysis: accounting, law, and consulting.

---

[2] Schumpeter (1934).

1.1.1 Accountants Diversify as Auditing Declines

Accountants diversify as their core business—auditing—shrinks, fundamentally changing their business mix. Many basic audit functions are being taken over by information technology. In particular when enhanced by artificial intelligence (AI) and deep learning, this becomes a very powerful tool for verifying company information and delivering near-ready audit reports. Human involvement can then be limited to making sure the software has done its job correctly, and to verifying exceptions and outliers. Fortunately, the demand for risk management and IT support has greatly increased and many accountants now earn their money mainly through consultancy.

A continuous stream of new regulatory requirements also provides extra work. But the bottom line is that we can see a structural decline in the number of smaller firms, which in many developed countries have been disappearing at a rate of 1–2% per year.[3]

Recruitment of "NewGen" staff is also a major challenge for accountants. Twenty percent of firms in Europe now point to the lack of junior recruits as the biggest obstacle to growth. Young accountants have different priorities from their predecessors. Among millennials—those born between 1980 and 2000 approximately—it appears that learning new things has the highest priority (90%), ahead of a good income (82%) and clear career expectations (71%). Accordingly, many of them do not even want to become partner and new accountants leave their firm at an annual rate of 17%.[4] For the older generations, this is unheard of and incomprehensible. Small firms give young accountants the opportunity to fulfill their social function in their own way and at their own pace.

The managing partner of one of these startups (The Independence Company) states: "With us, the accountants are self-employed. They are involved for part of the year in audit assignments for the large firms, while the rest of the year should be fun, dedicated to advisory assignments that are generally off-limits to auditors."

Most accounting firms have therefore responded to these challenges by diversifying first into tax advice and later into consulting work and legal advice (see Fig. 1.1). Their success in these expansions is based on their office locations that span the globe, their brands, and in many cases their office networks. The big four accountants have become huge multinationals, larger than many comparable business services companies.

The big four full-service accountants and other major firms will continue to exist because they have clients and projects that need a large international audit and/or consultancy network. And their clients accept the associated high costs.

The boutique firms that emerge on the edges will undoubtedly maintain and increase their market position thanks to low costs and frequently with the help of IT. In between, we have a middle group of smaller international and national firms. It is this group that is facing the greatest challenge to its existence.

---

[3] NL Bankruptcy Register.
[4] Rabobank Professional Sector Report (2018).

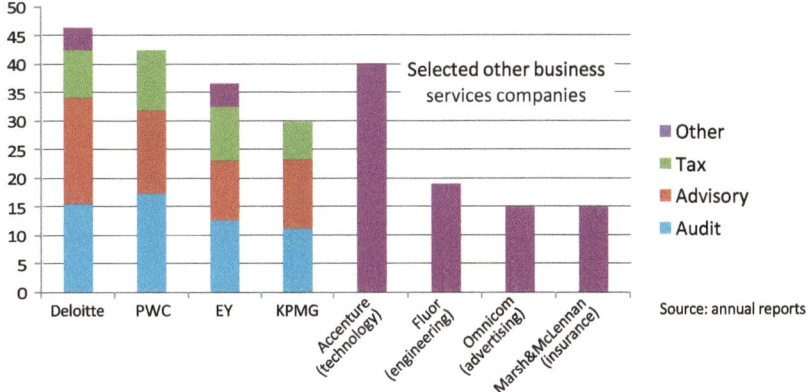

Fig. 1.1 Worldwide revenues of "big four" accounting firms

1.1.2 Lawyers Automate as They Specialize

At the same time, the number of lawyers at the larger firms is slowly decreasing too, by around 1% per year.[5] This decline is particularly strong among junior staff who are most vulnerable to substitution by ICT and low-cost competition. Leverage (i.e., number of juniors per partner) is going down, as the following graph shows for the USA (see Fig. 1.2).

As the senior partner of a law firm from the port city of Rotterdam explains: "If you look at the market, more and more players are sharing the same cake. There are simply too many firms and lawyers, margins are getting smaller and there is strong disruption from digitization. You then see the reactions: merge, close the shop, collaborate more or continue autonomously. Our firm can maintain its independence because we have a real niche, in our case a leading position in transport, logistics and international trade."

Lawyers will also increasingly move into areas that are not purely legal and are traditionally served by consultants and accountants (see Fig. 1.3). Some have started auditing the ethics of their clients; others examine the policies and actions of the management of a large bank, or start an independent tax practice.[6] Others have joined one of the larger accountancy

---

[5] US Bureau of Labor Statistics.
[6] Smets et al. (2012).

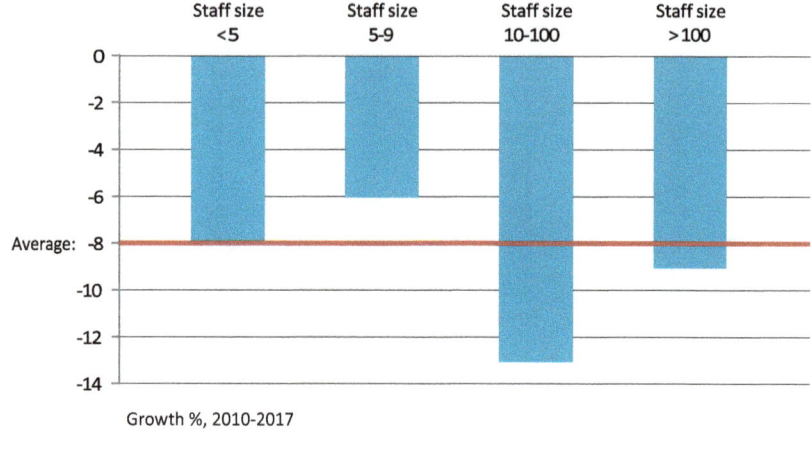

Fig. 1.2 Decrease in law offices in the USA

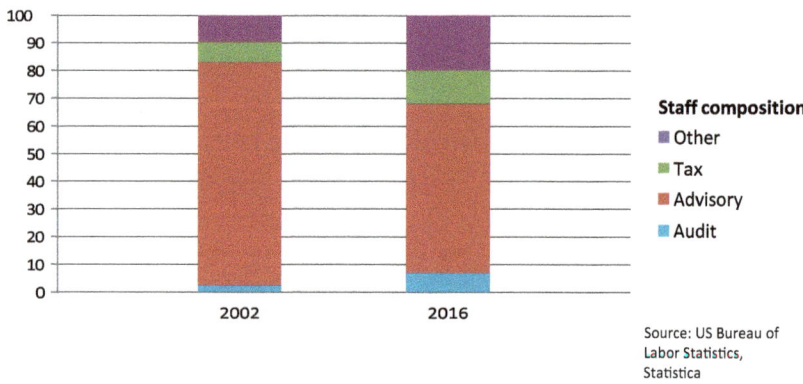

Fig. 1.3 Increasing differentiation in law firms

groups that are energetically embracing law: PWC, Deloitte, and EY, for example, are rapidly growing their legal staff.

But it is striking that simply expanding internationally does not automatically lead to market success, as the numbers show. Examples are Allen & Overy (London), Baker McKenzie (Chicago), and Dentons

(Beijing and Washington). Apart from their home market and a small number of rapidly developing regions, their offices are stagnating and, in some cases, even shrinking.

The medium-sized national firms that are successful show that good positioning and the associated reputation, together with a solid business model, are more important than being part of an international company or having an ambitious expansion program. A series of medium-sized firms and boutiques focus on areas that are the core business of large firms. Specialized firms such as Wachtell Lipton Rosen & Katz (New York) and Simmons & Simmons (London) do more acquisition transactions than the more general firms. They are highly specialized and relatively cost-effective.

Large firms such as Allen & Overy nowadays respond with greater flexibility, including cost flexibility, in the form of a pool that partly consists of former staff members. And reputation protects the big established names. To quote the managing partner of a Magic Circle firm in the City: "Clients that have the option of going to alternative service providers choose us because of convenience and the confidence that our name inspires. And we are able to take charge of a complex project, which we like to do. In the long term, the legal profession will become more like accountancy. A few (3–5) large firms, many boutiques, and between them a number of firms that are trying to achieve success through clear positioning in a specific practice or client area. The firms in the middle are stuck, being too small for full service, too large for a specialty boutique."

The case of a European local—Kienhuis Hoving—exemplifies the challenge: "After a rebound in 2016, our firm's turnover declined by 7.7% from €15.7 to €14.5 million. The firm is in transition," says managing partner Frans Van der Vaart. "My mission is to have us change course," he says. "Until recently, the partnership had many older partners phasing out from the age of sixty, a few more will follow later this year. The structure of the partner group has not been very balanced, but we now have several young talents and new partners."

He believes that changing track is easier for large firms with ample resources, but also sees a business case for a regional firm such as KienhuisHoving. "Listed companies are thin on the ground in our more rural area. Municipalities as a rule no longer use one law firm. There are nice start-ups and spin-offs from the local university but they will quickly move west when they grow. How can we win their loyalty? We try to tailor our services to their problems, but that is not easy. These are all conditions that force us to become more innovative, while our hourly rates remain attractive. There is still a lot of market available to us. But our partner structure, as with many medium-sized firms, works like a fleet of oil tankers that can only change course with great difficulty."

1.1.3 Consultants Threaten to Lose Focus

Many advisors seem lost when trying to understand what is happening and are asking themselves what kind of profession they actually are. The days are gone when the consultant could rely on superior knowledge and insight in the field of strategy, organization, or automation. Competition is closing in from all directions. For example, consultants used to be the preferred source of strategic creative ideas. Nowadays, that function is offered to the client in entirely new ways by designers, data specialists, artists, and many other professions. Consultants used to have a highly profitable side business in conducting reviews of management effectiveness or ethics. The former activity is now being penetrated by accountancies and recruitment firms and the latter by law firms. Simultaneously, the profession is fragmenting. The leader of a consumer goods company no longer calls McKinsey for every bit of business advice but turns to retailing specialists Horwath for strategy, Simon Kucher for pricing analysis, and NPS Lab for media analysis. Companies close to or in bankruptcy like Lehman Brothers and Enron no longer call a large multiservice consultancy but experts like Alvarez & Marsal or AlixPartners. These are all effective and efficient experts in their own area. The customer is no longer satisfied with advice without commitment, but expects hands-on implementation support and participation in the business risk. Today, an estimated 15 to 20% of assignments in Europe are already carried out in a non-traditional way, a percentage that is continuing to increase gradually, says Thomas Lünendonk, Senior Partner of the German consulting firm Lünendonk & Hossenfelder and publisher of the annual *Consulting Handbook*. It is therefore no surprise that a recent survey showed that consultants see new entrants, including small boutiques and freelancers, as a serious threat. If only because these appear to be more successful in recruiting promising new juniors, which nowadays is their biggest challenge.

These trends have consequences. In the last few years, firms such as Booz, Braxton, and Monitor have disappeared from the roster of large international agencies. Large national firms can only survive through reorientation and restructuring. The Managing Partner of Berenschot, a large European consultancy, noted in 2017: "Clients ask us to… focus less on analysis and more on realization. The lead times of projects are shorter… The existential issues of organizations are much more acute … In addition, the natural knowledge advantage that consultants used to have over their clients has disappeared. After all, clients now go to the same business schools as their advisors." Two years later, the same firm appointed a new Managing Partner who announced a change of direction from consulting to training and masterclasses: "Clients want consulting firms to help solve their problems. That means that they also want access to our knowledge. We have therefore decided to let them see behind the scenes."

A director of a multinational corporation puts it as follows: "MBB (read: McKinsey, BCG, Bain) prefer transformation to strategy as the projects and revenues per client are much larger. The theme now is *end to end*—as in *idea to market* or *order to cash*." This is unattractive for ambitious juniors because the implementation work tends to be monotonous. But good and reliable consultancy work with excellent account management will of course continue to exist as a profession if it is linked to a strong brand. Cees Bijl, chief strategist at healthcare multinational Philips, adds: "External consultants remain a very attractive option because—unlike Philips' own people—they only do 1-2 projects at a time and therefore have focus, in addition to relevant expertise. And because they can be deployed flexibly and at short notice. But for expertise, we now use our own people or freelancers, and for creativity we seek out a design firm. For change management we often look for combinations, such as McKinsey with Deloitte or PWC with Accenture."

A German senior partner from an international full-service accountancy firm summarizes it this way: "Consultancy is now primarily becoming a transformation business. The analytical function—with exception of creative thinking—is becoming a commodity and is taken over by artificial intelligence while routine tasks are outsourced to low-wage nations. Because of these developments, the master/ apprentice relationship at the firm is threatened. This is an increasing problem."

The major consultancies counter these trends with acquisition strategies that target small and innovative boutiques to broaden their skills base. For example, McKinsey has made a series of acquisitions of smaller innovative firms in recent years, including QuantumBlack (advanced analytics, London), LUNAR (design, Silicon Valley) Aberkyn (the Netherlands, training/coaching—an original spin-off that the company bought back), VLT Labs (digital product engineering anddesign, Malta), and Eggsplore (Belgium). Digital-McKinsey and McKinsey Solutions emerged from its own practice, as did McKinsey Analytics, McKinsey Implementation Services, and McKinsey Transformation Services. Accenture has set aside €1.5 billion for expansion in new business areas and has in recent years made more than five acquisitions per year of innovative firms. The full-service accountancies have followed and have bought into strategy consulting: PWC by taking over Booz Allen, Deloitte by buying Monitor, and EY by acquiring a number of offices of OC&C. The regional and national consultancy firms are feeling the pressure. Most of them complain about strong price pressure and competition from both large multinationals and small, maneuverable, and cost-effective boutiques. This increasingly leaves the clients confused as to what they are buying: focused cost-effective competencies or access to a broad multiservice network.

One consequence of these considerations is that success in the consulting world depends more than ever on clarity about the value proposition that the firm offers. There is no room any more for fuzziness and shifts in positioning. Firms must set priorities and choose one of three routes: opting for expertise and innovation, emphasizing superior client insight and client contact, or distinguishing themselves through efficiency and low cost.[7] Incidentally, the use of a new business model can sometimes enable a company to be at the forefront of all three for a time.[8] Many large firms do not seem to have a clear and unambiguous answer to these challenges. The following diagram illustrates this conundrum.

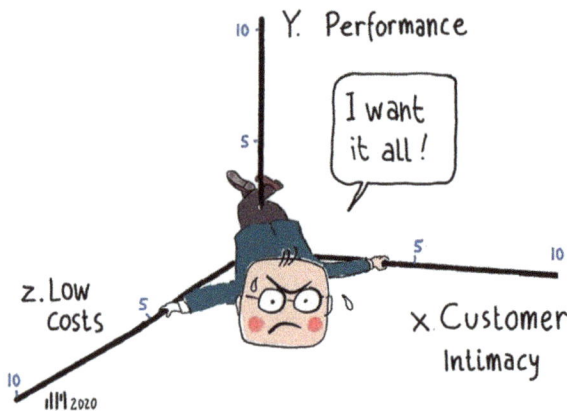

> **Repair the roof**
>
> …while the sun shines: a sensible thing to do. It is an obvious truth that you should use the profits of a business upturn when you can afford the investment to prepare your firm for the future. These years are not bad for business, notwithstanding the sharp downturn due to the COVID-19 crisis. But if the economy picks up again, our professions will continue to flourish. So, if we want to prepare for the future, why not do it now? Strangely enough, this obvious logic is out of synch with what we see in the real world.
>
> **Against all logic**
>
> We professionals have become used to the fact that our recommendations, packed with rational truth, are often not followed by our valued clients: an array of other interventions is often needed to get our client to the point where he follows what is evidently the best way forward. Let us call it resistance to change or—as economists discovered belatedly—the fact that there is more between heaven and earth than logic. Oddly enough, professionals show the same peculiarities, and we often fail to follow our own advice! As in "The shoemaker's children go barefoot." With today's disrup-
>
> *(continued)*

---

[7] Volberda et al. (2018).
[8] Treacy and Wiersema (1985).

(continued)

tions and major changes in professional services, a proactive attitude and adequate reaction would be appropriate. And after the shake-out of the last crisis, one would expect the surviving firms to be busy rethinking their strategies and models. Will the COVID-19 crisis be a wake-up call to make us think more proactively about the future? Alas, following previous recessions, most firms got right back down to business as usual without substantial change. The attitude was often one of: "it will last me out!"

The future is different

So—how active are you and your firm in working toward a future in the digital world, with buzzwords such as big data and artificial intelligence a sign of major changes to come? What are you really doing to attract and keep bright young people with different values to your firm? Are you actively reassessing relationships with your clients and discussing new arrangements with them, such as co-makership and pay for performance?

These kinds of changes in your traditional way of doing business can lead to a substantial rethink of the procedures, organization, and attitudes of your firm. They may well call for substantial investment and entail unusual risks. Everybody can learn, but changing behavior is one of the most difficult skills to master. And of course, these are topics that horrify older generations: people who have their retirement in sight and their pension taken care of. Like the senior partners of your firm perhaps?

Don't rock the boat

Most partners don't really worry about the future of their profession and their firm. Perhaps the managing partner does, but he or she has enough difficulty getting the partners' attention for more pressing operational matters. Which staff members, when the topic does not interest them, don't happily remind themselves that leadership jobs are usually rotated in their firm: the irksome Managing Partner won't last long… So, they are busy with clients and assignments, which is of course ok, but also explains why it is so difficult to embark on a real change project in traditional professional organizations. Since we are talking with intelligent people, we should not be surprised to find a lot of understanding of the strategic challenges ahead. But when they are asked to take charge and make a move, the answer is "changes are slow; no need to be first; this will last" and "there'll be time enough to act."

Looking in the mirror

There is no quick fix, no magic remedy for this conundrum. Instead, there is curiosity in seeing the contradiction between partners who act decisively and rapidly within their client organizations and the same partners who procrastinate when it concerns their own firm. A union foreman once told me that I should not make the mistake of thinking that the demands he made of his employers would be applicable to his own union organization. Since then I have added the treatment of schizophrenia to my toolkit as a consultant.

You are crazy to want to repair your roof when the sun is shining! Enjoy the sun and dream on!

1.2 The Four Major Disruptions of Our Professional Existence

In our own life as a lawyer, accountant, or consultant, the demand for our services and how we deliver them is changing considerably.[9] We can divide the causes of these creeping—but still serious—disruptions into four categories: (i) information and communication technology, which enables and requires radically different ways of working; (ii) the "new generation"—professionals who want to work in a different way and want to make their career on their own terms; (iii) the constant pressure from our critical clients to deliver the best performance for progressively lower budgets; and (iv) the increasing complexity of the issues that clients refer to their professional advisors, which often require them to combine deep expertise with a top-level helicopter perspective.

1.2.1 Technology Disrupts

In a world where a great deal of knowledge can be found through the Internet and smart software, fewer and fewer clients see the added value of professional support for more routine work. One example: Deloitte takes the lead and announces that the first 20-odd of its 160 audit packages are 100% digitally checked for all its clients, "i.e. on an industrial scale," confirms the head of accounting practice. Another example: Lex

---

[9] Smets et al. (2017).

Machina, a subsidiary of publisher Relx Group, uses an algorithm that scans PDFs of legal jurisprudence and related documentation.[10] This helps a lawyer prepare for his or her pitch to win the assignment, for the court case and for the mediation, at a much lower cost. Half of all US law firms now use the services of Lex Machina in their work. Charley Moore, Organizer/CEO of Rocket Lawyer in San Francisco: "Legal support is incredibly expensive and most consumers and smaller companies cannot afford to conclude proper contracts. Rocket Lawyer makes that affordable by using powerful information technology. This is a huge new market. And remote work technology gives home-based people an opportunity to operate as fully fledged professionals."[11] In Europe, we see this at consumer level: retailer Tesco has twenty legal products on the shelf. Firms that provide only routine legal advice are having an increasingly hard time.

The Internet is becoming a key pillar of our economy, and perhaps even the most important driver of progress. According to Deloitte, the Internet sector already provides more jobs in the Netherlands than the construction industry, for example.[12] Knowledge and access to knowledge are losing their value as a distinguishing quality of professionals, who are still having trouble in convincingly demonstrating their real

compared to this...

T-rex is a pussycat

---

[10] McGinnis and Pearce (2014).
[11] Fried and Heinemeier Hansson (2013).
[12] McAfee and Brynjolfsson (2012).

added value. With the further development of IT-related services, the required competencies of professionals are changing.[13]

In our field we still carry out all kinds of repetitive work that will be automated," says the chairman of Alfa Accountants and Advisors. "We will increasingly rely on the deep learning skills of our computers to look up the professional literature, analyze financial statements and run our meetings.[14]

Many older professionals/partners can no longer or will not adapt.

The result is a drop in demand and the emergence of new startups. IT makes a completely new way of working possible. René Seyger, senior partner at Roland Berger strategy consultants, concludes:

> **The information paradox**
>
> Nowadays, information is ubiquitous—every item is instantly available anywhere. No need to read a book or open a journal. A few clicks on a search engine will deliver any knowledge that the reader might need. This is certainly true for "management stuff," be it data on markets, facts about technologies, or concepts of business theory. And nearly all of it is free, too. And when you want to tally up your numbers and present them elegantly, just load Excel and PowerPoint, and off you go. Sounds like the end of knowledge workers like you and me, doesn't it? Let's see how it works in practice.
>
> **Doing fine**
>
> I recently had the opportunity to discuss this with a young doctor. He told me how he deals with patients who find answers to a lot of their questions online before seeing him. First, he asks them what they have found out about their complaint on the Internet. He is then given all kinds of information, some of it true, some of it dangerous nonsense, some of it relevant, and sometimes even new information. This is the start of his conversation with the patient. He explains and structures the information the patient has found and puts it in perspective. He weeds out the useless and helps focus on the important facts of the patient's specific problem. At the end of this "coaching" session, diagnosis and cure emerge as a logical conclusion. It is a beautiful example of a professional dealing with the new reality, while continuing to add substantive value.
>
> *(continued)*

---

[13] Susskind and Susskind (2015), Susskind (2017).
[14] Hinings et al. (2018).

(continued)
Another example: project management is one of the best-known and most well-documented management tools. The essentials are already taught at high schools. Nonetheless, courses and workshops on project management remain popular and professional societies that discuss the latest application technique are flourishing. There is apparently a gap between knowing a topic and using the skill in practice.
The key is mastering the right application!
The paradox? On one hand, there is the ease with which we can inform ourselves about a methodology and find the data to make it work. On the other hand, there is the challenge of achieving success with our approach. An abundance of information leads to laziness, as the basic facts are quickly gathered and the analysis is sloppy. There is no interest in background or fundamentals. Implementation is not considered until it is time to take action. And then one discovers that it is too late and there is no connection between the method used and the situation at hand. Fruitful implementation becomes a mission impossible.
As a management consultant, one is asked for advice about "process management" or "agile development." When digging into the problem, you may find the client lost in methodology after having followed a management fad, and without any connection between method and problem.
Knowledge changes!
In conclusion, this is good news for professionals who want to stay in business. They need to change the way they use knowledge for their practice and stop relying on readily available information which will not be perceived as adding value to their contribution. Instead, they should focus on selecting and applying those methods that do add value to the specific case at hand. And they should of course use insightful information where needed to support the method. This requires a deep understanding of the client's problem and of the method, including how the latter will solve the former. Professionals can therefore demonstrate their value by applying their experience and wisdom. And, by the way: advise your client to use a good e-learning course to become acquainted with the basics of your method. He will appreciate it!

The partner remains important because of his/her deep sense of the client's situation, his/her personal relationships and interface with the AI machine. But at the same time, we are seeing the end of the classic consultancy model.[15]

---

[15] Van der Mandele (2004).

1.2.2 New Generations: A Different Breed of Professional

Young professionals who have a different lifestyle and who are a little less monomaniacal in organizing their lives than previous generations are an important driving force for change.[16] They no longer want to work an indecent number of hours a week, unless they can clearly see the immediate benefits. And they are less money and career-conscious. They relate their ambitions to broader work values such as environment and sustainability. They are less loyal to the firm, change jobs with more ease, and are less prone to sign up for a long-term partnership track. All these tendencies threaten the structure of the traditional firm. "The idea that you have a good job when you work for a prestigious company dates from around 1880 to 1980," *The Economist* noted not long ago. The managing partner of a large accounting firm confirms: "New generations of professionals no longer want to work hard for ten years to become a partner. This puts our income model and the associated leverage under pressure."[17]

According to a survey by the Young Lawyers Association of the Netherlands (SJBN Foundation), more than 55% of lawyers in the Netherlands complain about a poor work–life balance. More than one-third of respondents regularly consider resigning from their law firm.[18] The results of the survey show that having the option of more flexible working hours improves retention. Young accountants have a similar reaction to their working conditions. In a recent study by Nyenrode University, 37% of the young accountants surveyed found that they had a skewed relationship between work, study, and leisure. To quote one of the respondents: "My employment contract states my working week to be 40 hours, while my workload for the week amounts to 60 hours. This results in a working week of 80 hours."

---

[16] Noury et al. (2017), Smets et al. (2017).
[17] Kipping et al. (2019).
[18] Gilson and Mnookin (1989).

Miss Anna – I am a bit old fashioned you know. And I need you in the office – now!

To quote Jan Hommen, former CFO of Philips, former CEO of ING and from 2014 interim CEO of KPMG in the Netherlands for several years: "Young professionals undoubtedly want more freedom and flexibility. They are also, more than their predecessors, willing to invest in the future of themselves and the community around them."[19]

1.2.3 What Do the New Generations Want?

We can summarize a multitude of wishes in four dimensions:

1. A continuous learning experience with
2. A better work–life balance
3. More accountability and faster results, which
4. Take society and the environment into account.

---

[19] Dent et al. (2008).

A learning experience means varied work with different assignments and more variation in the career path. Better balance between work and private life means that an employee is no longer willing to audit the same files for the same client for ten years in order to become partner. Faster results mean a more rapid transfer to other tasks and/or more responsibility, as well as clear feedback from seniors, with commensurate rewards for success. Taking account of society and the environment means that the firm must have a vision of its role in society and the environment, and should act accordingly, preferably taking into account the sustainable development goals. All this goes a lot further than just making a profit. It takes time for senior partners to get used to their staff refusing to give up their parenting day when there is a rush project and being unwilling to interrupt their holidays to help their client out in an emergency.

The European Association of Accountancy concludes that the recruitment problems in accountancy will be solved if offices:

- Provide better coaching through more contact with the partners and more contact with the client
- Allow a better work–life balance in the job
- Create more challenges by offering a greater variety of work with fewer "checklist" jobs
- Strive for more social orientation
- Pay people for their performance rather than their hours
- Develop a broader vision with more social input

> **Are the NewGens getting or giving?**
>
> Somewhat presumptuous for a baby boomer to write about the true nature of the new generations, eh? But we cannot avoid the subject when thinking about the future of professional services. After all, our future and our present depend on those bright-eyed, bushy-tailed youngsters. But are they so different from their forebears? Unfortunately, I tend to think so, and this has a major impact on our profession and our firms. Reason enough to discuss the topic.

(continued)

(continued)

Going all out for your career!
Admittedly, I hail from a time when a career was a basic necessity of life. It included status symbols such as a comfortable home, the proper brand of car, and holidays to bucket-list resorts. In my days, the job was the main activity—maybe even the main thing in life. Our agenda: the firm, 24/7 if needed. Part-time or not work-related: never heard of it. Evenings spent in business or service clubs or politics—any networking activity that supported our professional future. The focus was on building our career. A growing practice, increasingly important assignments, more and more billings. Private life? A partner who was at least supposed to agree with this life and the income it entailed, while taking care of kids, house, and the wider family.

Times are changing…
Not long ago, my son said to me: "Dad, you didn't raise me, but I will do so with my own sons!" A painful truth. Which brings us to the differences between generations. Our offspring are simply not willing to invest most of their life in their job and career.

While a baby boomer would never worry about their job requiring sacrifice, younger generations see their lives in much broader terms. They embrace being parents—including the fathers!—and are happy to change diapers. I never did… They introduce anomalies such as Father's Day and flexible vacations. And even pursue the idea of a four-day working week. Weekends are sacred, reserved for family life. Work during evening hours? Tennis with partner and friends has blocked the diary! And why accept an unpaid charity board position that may involve a lot of work outside office

(continued)

(continued)

hours? Even the firm's summer BBQ is suspect. Should I really join people I often see at work? Of course, we are passionate about our work. But within strict limits...

Do I have a moral opinion about this? Certainly not! I understand and even sympathize with this view on life and work. But it does have major impact on the professions and the way in which they are organized.

And so, our professions are disrupted

It is not difficult to see the effects of this trend around us. To mention the main hurdles that are coming up.

Succession: today, many firms face problems with succession. Talented seniors no longer want to become partner in the firm. Once seen as "heaven on earth," it is now regarded as a chore to be avoided if at all possible. Why should I take care of others and even try to lead them when I can sit in our corner with our own interesting projects and clients? Why should I invest money and run the risk of not getting my payout in the end? Why should I want to be an entrepreneur when I picked this job to be a professional?

Acquisition: selling and keeping the pipe-line full, not only for oneself but also for the team and the firm, is not the favorite activity of most professionals. And if my reward is a coveted partner's seat that I don't value that much anymore, why should I engage in commercial work? Better if others do it. But who will keep sales going and stacks smoking in the long run?

Marketing and networking: developing the firm's market position and building an individual professional status is necessary for long-term survival. But it also takes time and competes with billable work, and of course one's private life. Some new-generation professionals just do not see the necessity of this longer-term development. And in some firms, it is noticeable that this important function is deteriorating.

Getting. And not giving

Frankly, I feel that there is a growing imbalance between the providing and receiving side of professions. It appears that the whole concept of personal investment in one's profession is vanishing. In my view, a rich and rewarding professional life has to be built over many years and should never be taken for granted. Are new generations spoiled? Or is this simply a temporary phenomenon that will readjust itself with the next recession? Or is this a fundamentally new way in which new generations will run their professions? Perhaps the crisis caused by COVID-19 is already having an as yet unknown impact!

(continued)

(continued)

1.2.4 Critical Clients Find New Solutions

Clients are becoming increasingly emancipated in their drive for more performance at a lower cost. Many of them have enjoyed the same education as the professionals that they employ and loyalty to their trusted firms is disappearing. Purchasing departments with a keen eye on cost–benefit ratios have been given an important role. Clients are no longer willing to pay the higher fees of a larger outfit because they no longer see the added value. Internal departments for legal affairs, auditing, and organizational advice with perfect knowledge of your company are becoming available—and at low costs. Lloyd Blankfein, Chairman of Goldman Sachs, concludes: "When I started, banks were wont to rely entirely on external law firms. Nowadays, our own legal department is the real advisor to our Board of Directors."

In public organizations, procurement rules play an important role in the pursuit of lower costs, with a pernicious effect on the quality and continuity of professional services. As a result, large firms with a high cost structure, such as Deloitte and EY, are withdrawing from the local government markets, for example. Their position is being taken over by smaller and low-cost accountants.

"General consultancy is dead," says the director of a fast-growing innovative strategy agency. Analytical cleverness does not have enough added value. Classic consulting teams only have value for a limited number of jobs, such as cost reduction. It is all about adding value. Large companies with high rates and large teams no longer do that. Too many detailed analyses. Insufficient insight. The managing partner of a law firm believes: "Every dollar spent on new-style legal work is worth as much as three dollars in traditional law. For a third of the costs, newcomers provide the same services as the old firms." Clients are looking for a clear proposition. To quote the CFO/COO of a national law firm: "You see a big hunt going on for work at the C-level of large corporations. We can only survive by focusing on other markets."

1.2.5 Surviving Complexity

The fourth disruptive development that will hit our business is a consequence of the increasing scope and complexity of our clients' business. Nowadays, our clients are no longer simple hierarchical workshops and their complexity has in many cases grown beyond the parable of the six blind men and the elephant.[20] Rather, we can now talk about a team of blind experts and a client octopus.

---

[20] John Godfrey Saxe: "IT was six men of Indostan, to learning much inclined, who went to see the elephant (though all of them were blind), that each by observation, might satisfy his mind…."

Gone are the days when accountants such as KPMG had both multinationals and local plumbers as clients; when consultants such as Arthur D. Little claimed that "everything is our business"; when lawyers such as Cravath Swain & Moore had a corporate as well as a family law practice. So, if you want to get ahead, you specialize.

Many are the options. The main directions:

- Industrial/application specialization—examples: media, technology, resources, industry
- Functional specialization—examples: finance, taxes, processes
- Geographic specialization at local, regional, national, or even global level
- Account specialization

The size of many of our professional interventions nowadays requires not a small team of actors at one location, but hundreds of managers and supporters across the globe. And our service no longer consists of the delivery of a single report, a contract, or an audit document, but rather the conclusion of a complex transaction, the introduction of a new system, or a complete transformation of an organization. Good ideas and their seamless implementation.[21]

Client complexity...

But these developments have created two competing demands on our professionals. On the one hand, the increasing complexity and scope of

---

[21] Van der Mandele (2006).

clients' activities are leading to more and more specialization. Our clients no longer ask for a corporate lawyer, but for an expert in entertainment industry acquisitions, international intellectual property, or US litigation. They no longer ask for a capable auditor, but for an expert on risk assessment, whitewashing, or computer audits. They no longer want a good organization consultant, but an expert on 6 Sigma, SAP implementation, or a leadership coach. With growing specialization, professionals increasingly end up being experts who deliver very specific knowledge and experience in a complex organization. As result, we are often no longer in a position to judge the value of our contribution and how it fits in the process as a whole, and we no longer see that as our task or responsibility. Management within the client organization takes care of that, right or wrong.

Try to add value to a complex client...

Furthermore, in a world where information and knowledge are increasingly ubiquitous and instant, it is becoming increasingly difficult to distinguish oneself both from competitors and from sources inside client organizations. An obvious choice, then, is to go for even more specialization, which makes professions more limited for the client and less interesting for many professionals. In conclusion, professions are narrowing to "one-trick pony" specialisms, driven by the growing availability of knowledge. And professionals who can repair the arm of the octopus, while understanding how it works as part of the whole animal, are becoming increasingly scarce.

However, large assignments nowadays can often be described as complete renewal of all or parts of the organization, where professionals are too seldom asked to consider all the aspects which need to be addressed for complete and sustainable results.

To make sure that professionals contribute to the positive outcome of large processes, clients have reached for two solutions. One is to split up the scope, define the quality, and minimize the cost of delivering the service by issuing tenders resulting in detailed delivery specifications. More often than not, these tenders eventually result in a downward spiral of rates and quality. And in a situation where no party oversees the whole change process. The other solution is to demand that the professionals cover many aspects and then carry part of the risk of their intervention. The simplest way could be through a bonus scheme, or in any case through an equity participation.

To achieve real results, however, our highly specialized professionals need to have a holistic view of their client organization and its business, social, and political environment. This is a tall order, and the way a client can achieve sustainable results is to seek longer term partnerships with trusted professional organizations which realize that their success ultimately depends on the success of their client. The solution for the professional is to find a way to combine two conflicting mindsets and skill sets in their team: the experts and the integrators who can show the way from

---

Focus—a devil of a conundrum

For as long as I have been a consultant, focus has been one of my big worries. The Germans have a wonderful phrase: "In der Beschränking zeigt sich der Meister," which means that we can only excel by limiting our field of activity. We cannot master every subject and we cannot be an expert in every profession. We can only acquire in-depth knowledge and produce high quality by limiting ourselves. But isn't this self-evident? It sounds crazy not to aspire to this. So why don't we see every good professional following this best practice?

Speak for yourself!

There is no need to explain the advantages of a focused practice. You already know it because you have heard about it in your business training and management courses. You have read about it in professional magazines.

(continued)

(continued)
Your boss has pointed it out in your job appraisals. You have seen the successes of your colleagues and competitors. You have noticed that clients prefer professionals with in-depth experience in their chosen field. After all, they go for track record, in particular if it has been realized over an extended period.

Or is there another truth?

The real disadvantages of a professional focus are not often mentioned. For starters, a lot of our thinking is subject to fashion. With time, many ideas and tools of the trade have lost their glamour. Who remembers "learning organization" or "7-S"? What about total quality management or business process engineering? With Agile projects as the next candidate. Some skills have been taken over by the client who no longer needs his trusted external advisor.

You had a flourishing practice on a fashionable theme and a professional network to help you along. And suddenly, the value has gone. Your focus was brilliant and it worked so well. But a few years later, the game is over. In the end, your focus got you nowhere.

Many of us have experienced this trauma when their beloved topic has disappeared. Or when their home market has declined:

"We only work for local government," or "Our heart lies in non-profit."

Is there a way out?

Of course, now you want to hear the solution to this dilemma: to focus or not to focus. Unfortunately, there is no holy grail in this quest. The way out appears to be to revisit the topic with a certain regularity in the course of your work. Focus if the conditions are right, "milk the market" when it offers the opportunity. But be aware of the risks; stay tuned to early signals that things are changing: the business journals discuss a new theme, your job applicants ask for a new skill, a loyal client suddenly invites a new competitor.

How difficult it is to be in time, and to be prepared for the next era! The routines that you have perfected in recent years—your consulting "machine"—have been optimized to deliver the best quality for the least effort. And it has limited—if any—flexibility for other work.

A sensible professional entrepreneur teams up with people who are skilled in focus areas of the future. And there are some—but not many—"ambidextrous" professionals who enjoy doing their legacy work by day, while exploring the new practice in the evening. Lucky you, because it is much more fun to run a hybrid practice than to be limited to a single focus.

And now you have your own reason to try to excel in different professional areas at the same time! Right?

blueprint to implementation.[22] The community of professional firms that is described in this book is the perfect model for combining these to create a different way of working in our firms and with our clients.

1.3 Current Strategies Will Not Help

The trends mentioned above, individually but also taken together, provide a strong impetus to seek other paths. Disruption is striking many parts of our business model. The "brain power"—the engine that determines the essential value of the firm—will in future have to be provided by critical, independent, and entrepreneurial young people who have their own view of their career and the organization. We have seen above how our clients are changing, and with them the range of services that they need: fewer reports with smart perspectives on business figures, legal problems, and markets. More ability to harness complex databases and smart software with effective and risk-sharing support for the ensuing change processes. As a result, our clients' expectations for our earnings model are also changing. Fewer hourly fees. More project tenders and service subscriptions on the one hand; more risk-sharing and equity participation on the other.

Do I really need a consultant or lawyer again?

---

[22] Drucker (1999).

The competencies that are expected from our people are also changing dramatically. We need talent to find and summarize data, and the capacity to deal with large databases and smart software. We also need the capability to integrate the information and knowledge thus gained in order to obtain results for the client in a team setting. This requires social intelligence and leadership.

The owners and partners of our firms today must handle difficult dilemmas. Some of the questions:

- What is the impact of these trends on our own firm and its practice?
- How do we remain attractive to clients who continuously ask for more results and specialization at a lower cost?

We have to find coherent and future-proof answers to questions like this. And we will: just read on!

References

Christensen, C. M., & Overdorf, M. (2000). Meeting the challenge of disruptive change. *Harvard Business Review, 78*(May-April), 66–72.
Dent, F., Holton, V., & Rabbetts, J. (2008). *Motivation and employee engagement in the 21st century*. Ashridge Management Index.
Drucker, P. F. (1999). Knowledge worker productivity: The biggest challenge. *California Management Review, 1*(2), 77–94.

Fried, J., & Heinemeier Hansson, D. (2013). *Remote: Office not required*. Random House.

Gilson, R., & Mnookin, R. (1989). Coming of age in a corporate law firm: The economics of associate career patterns. *Stanford Law Review, 41*, 567–595.

Hinings, B., Gegenhuber, T., & Greenwood, R. (2018). Digital innovation and transformation: An institutional perspective. *Information and Organization, 28*(1), 52–61.

Kipping, M., Bühlmann, F., & David, T. (2019). Professionalization through symbolic and social capital: Evidence from the careers of elite consultants. *Journal of Professions and Organization, 6*(3), 265–285.

McAfee, A., & Brynjolfsson, E. (2012). Big data: The management revolution. *Harvard Business Review, 90*(10), 60–68.

McGinnis, J. O., & Pearce, R. G. (2014). The great disruption, how machine intelligence will transform the role of lawyers in the delivery of legal services. *Fordham Law Review, 82*, 3041–3067.

Noury, L., Gand, S., & Sardas, J. C. (2017). Tackling the work-life balance challenge in professional service firms: The impact of projects, organizing, and service characteristics. *Journal of Professions and Organization, 4*(2), 149–178.

Schumpeter, J. A. (1934). *The theory of economic development: An inquiry into profits, capital, credit, interest and the business cycle*. Harvard University Press.

Smets, M., Morris, T., & Greenwood, R. (2012). From practice to field: A multilevel model of practice-driven institutional change. *Academy of Management Journal, 55*(4), 877–904.

Smets, M., Morris, T., von Nordenflycht, A., & Brock, D. M. (2017). 25 years since 'p2': Taking stock and charting the future of professional firms. *Journal of Professions and Organization, 4*(2), 91–111.

Susskind, R. (2017). *Tomorrow's lawyers: An introduction to your future* (2nd ed.). Oxford University Press.

Susskind, R., & Susskind, D. (2015). *The future of the professions: How technology will transform the work of human experts*. Oxford University Press.

Treacy, M., & Wiersema, F. (1985). *The discipline of market leaders: Choose your customers, narrow your focus, dominate your markets*. Perseus Books.

Van der Mandele, L. M. (2004). *Leadership and the inflection point, a longitudinal perspective*. Ph.D. Series Research in Management, ERIM, Rotterdam.

Van der Mandele, H. C. (2006). *Economic apoptosis and uncontrollability. A first enquiry into the concepts and their relevance for the market-government debate.* Diss., University of Groningen.

Volberda, H., Van den Bosch, F., & Heij, K. (2018). *Reinventing business models: How firms cope with disruption.* Oxford University Press.

Professionals will sell you anything!

2

Understanding How Professionals Work: Building Blocks for the Future

2.1 Understanding Our Business Model

Business model thinking was first introduced in the industrial world and has proven its value there in the past decade.[1,2] It has now taken hold of professional service firms.[3,4] Colleagues are looking at elements like value proposition, organizational structure, and partnerships when thinking about their future. This is quite helpful as long as one realizes that each firm has its unique character that calls for a unique design. Before piecing the model together we must first understand the way in which we can deliver value to our clients—what we can deliver and how we can deliver. And the ways in which we can be compensated for our services. We can illustrate these issues with the following diagram (see Fig. 2.1).

---

[1] Osterwalder and Pigneur (2010).
[2] Volberda et al. (2018).
[3] Van der Mandele and Parker (2009).
[4] Van der Mandele et al. (2019).

2.2 Services: What We Deliver

Professionals can offer an almost infinite range of services, from creative design to a carefully worded document, a good conversation, or the interim management of a factory. Not only are there many types of services, the content of our services is continuously changing due to external developments, both at the client level and within our own firm.

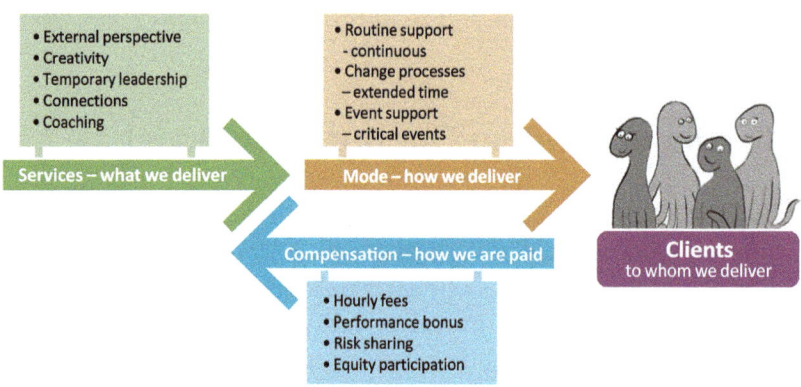

Fig. 2.1 Delivering value in professional services

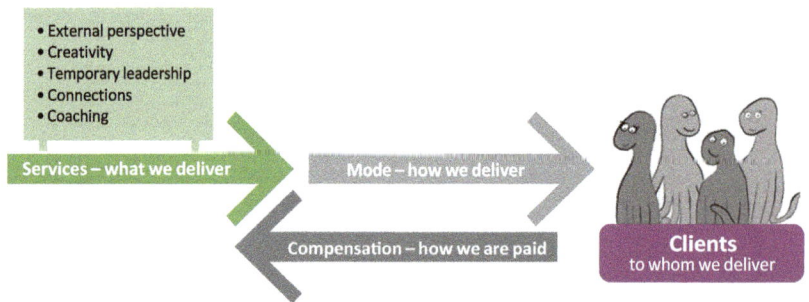

Fig. 2.2 What we deliver

2 Understanding How Professionals Work: Building Blocks...

If we want to understand what types of professional services are there, we can use our business model to analyze how our business is changing (see Fig. 2.2). To begin with we can distinguish five types of services. Professionals can deliver:

1. External perspective
2. Creativity
3. Temporary leadership
4. Connections
5. Coaching and trusted advice

2.2.1 External Perspective

This is the traditional role as a professional in which we are the source of expertise knowledge and even wisdom. Expertise is the ticket with which we traditionally earn our money. Our clients usually do not see more than they experience in their work and most of them are unable and have no time or interest to look beyond their current practice with their own juniors, their technology, and their clients. They all suffer from different levels of tunnel vision, subjectivity, and, at times, worrying prejudices. At that point it is a good idea to hire an expert who does not suffer from these deficiencies, who will report coolly what the business beyond his horizons look like, and what are the great unknowns. And that many emperors really do have no clothes—thus holding up the mirror that we all need. Wise clients are smart enough to pay for that!

That external perspective ranges from legislation and jurisprudence in law to regulations on company accounts and market insight in business. Not to mention the impact of technology on the professions. A lot is changing in the way expertise is delivered. In the past, junior attorneys searched library shelves for hours looking for the appropriate jurisprudence in support for their case.

Also a thing of the past are the days when the accountant checked journal entries with a red pencil and the consultant was on the road to conduct his own market research with face-to-face interviews. Online and that may be done with help of artificial intelligence has now taken over a good part of this work. As a result we need fewer juniors who can thus direct their attention to other tasks.

2.2.2 Creativity

If the client can no longer find a way out of a problem, an outside impulse can give a breakthrough. Someone who will propose a radically different approach and an unorthodox solution. A professional who thinks "out of the box" and who likes to put her or his teeth in your challenge. That one idea or that one new approach that can do wonders and prove to be invaluable. As more routine work disappears, professionals can concentrate on insoluble, complex, and "wicked" problems. And the demand for creative solutions is increasing, albeit that it is often met by non-traditional firms.

An example is Spark Optimus, a fast-growing consulting boutique that has emerged from McKinsey and uses many of the McKinsey traits but also successfully advertises itself as a team of young and creative consultants who invent new solutions for clients. Creativity starts with individual talent—thinking power—and is strongly supported by the right culture.

2.2.3 Leadership: Ad Interim

How nice and useful can it be for a client who has an emergency or a temporary gap in leadership to have someone from outside to take charge in his or her organization. Then he can take a step aside, as expertise,

Leadership – cross the Delaware

experience, and trust combine with an ability to take charge. Power and authority within limits, but still an increasing share of the professional market is taken by interim management in of all its forms.

2.2.4 Connections and Network

The mergers and alliances and the specialization of functions in corporations, the increases in hierarchy, and complexity—it all leads to disconnects that hamper teamwork within their organization. In many branches, we see a multitude of interlocking and interdependent organizations, multidimensional matrices, and a spaghetti of organizational units which are obliged to cooperate. The boundaries between units and people increase as firms/organizations grow, locally, internationally, and across practices. There are even nightmares of organizations that come to a standstill due to their own complexity. And so there are countless government departments, multinationals, and international organizations that suffer from the same management infarct. Poor communications, distrust, and information blockages dominate.[5] In such a situation, an external connector can do an excellent job by building bridges, enabling collaboration, and thus averting the infarct. The ability to connect is primarily a matter of professional skills. A supporting organization helps.

---

[5] Van der Mandele (2006).

On the road with your trusted advisor

2.2.5 Coach and Trusted Advice

Traditionally, organizations and their leaders use independent outsiders as sounding board for their decisions and to improve their way of working. If we coach a manager intensively we can end up in the position of "trusted advisor," based on our reputation or that of our firm, as well as our personal relationship. Above all, our client wants a neutral listening ear who will wag a warning finger when something goes wrong and we will report things that others are reluctant to mention. And our client wants a sounding board to reflect on his problems, fears, and visions. The engaged presence—of a person or a reputed professional or a reputed professional organization – gives the clients confidence in the chosen course.[6]

2.3 Three Ways to Deliver Professional Work

The different types of service described above can be offered broadly in three different ways—as routine support, as a longer term change process, and as event support (see Fig. 2.3).

First of all, a large part of professional services consists of *routine support* of organizational processes. Employees must be signed up with labor

---

[6] Maister et al. (2000).

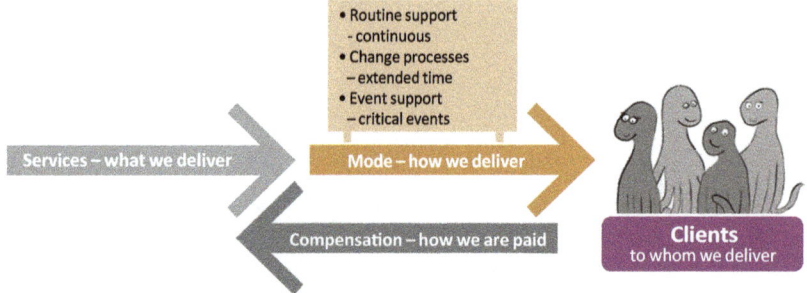

Fig. 2.3 Mode: how we deliver

contracts, annual revenues, costs, and earnings must be audited, and company articles of incorporation need to be updated from time to time. Many of these routine jobs will be automated in the future. We saw, to cite an example, that the workforce of the larger accounting firms is declining by 1.5 percent per annum. Many of these services can be supplied from databases of contracts, policies, and procedures, which can be made more accessible with artificial intelligence.

In addition, there are important *change processes* at organizations that often can only be achieved with significant external support and often take a year or longer. Examples are the implementation of mergers between companies, the introduction of heavy automation packages, or heavy cost reduction programs. These processes will continue to require a lot of manpower in the future.

Routine support by a trained professional

Finally, the support of professional firms is almost always called in during important strategic or organizational transitions. We are talking about *event support*, and that event may concern a takeover, a merger, or an important reorientation of the organization. This usually calls for legal and accounting expertise. And again ICT exerts its influence as the supervision of the event is taken over by the platform database that manages the entire process. An example are the data platforms that international law firms offer nowadays in support of major acquisitions.

Event support: big change, high risk, high trust – and high cost...

2.4 Compensation: How Professionals Are Paid

The traditional way to invoice your client for your professional services is by hourly fee. This concept has evolved over time (see Fig. 2.4). These days, the majority lawyers charge their client per 6-minute timeslot. Many consultants charge per hour or day, or even per week or month. Major engagements are sold by international strategy houses like McKinsey as monthly fee per team of 3–30 or more consultants. And, finally, an increasing number of professional services are now contracted as a lump sum-fixed fee, in which the provider bears the risk of

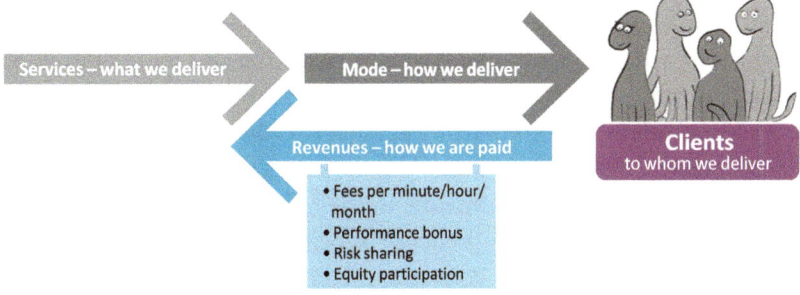

Fig. 2.4 How we are paid in professional services

overruns—which can be advantageous for himself if the time actually spent is less than budgeted. But at that point, the professional has started to carry risk which in this case is limited to his own cost. The next step is the success bonus that is paid out when the project results in a measured advantage for the client. The final step in risk-taking is reached when the professional takes an equity position in the project to which he contributes. Seniors in professional services note that there is a trend from low-risk fixed fees to risk-taking arrangements like performance bonuses and even equity participation. At that point by the way the border between professional services and private equity becomes vague, which explains why some professionals find it easy to make the career transfer to investment firms.

The result are trends visible on the one hand to fixed-priced or lump sum contracts and on the other to risk-sharing remuneration. Fixed-price contracts and tenders are becoming increasingly prevalent starting with the government work. In recent years, this has set professional services for municipalities and other government institutions on a downward spiral, in which fee reduction is followed by cost reduction and more risk-taking. Many firms have now left this market. Variable remuneration in the form of a success bonus continues its inexorable rise. Many firms now achieve 10–20 percent of their turnover from variable contracts. There are also firms that make capital investments in their clients' projects: the professional as an investing entrepreneur. Rebel Group is a good example of this.

Fig. 2.5 Risk and return of different professional service contracts

This firm with its head office in Rotterdam and branches in the USA, South Africa, and the Philippines is mainly concerned with infrastructural and environmental projects where its own capital is deployed. In such cases, the pay is much higher, but is largely received only after the work has been completed—sometimes many years after the end of the project. The resulting gap between the professional's income (expectation) and payment will usually have to be financed by the firm, while the risk can rise considerably. The following diagram illustrates the trends (see Fig. 2.5).

2.5 What Is Our Business Model?

The business model that determines the success of a professional organization works at three levels. The basis are the sources of professional value—like brainpower and knowledge. At the second level value is created by the organizations and its processes. And at the end, value is delivered in the form of services to clients.

Business starts with the *source of value* of our professional services. These are the basic resources that we need when we start working to deliver our services. In industry we would talk about raw materials and about labor and financing. In professional services, we can categorize:

- The *brainpower* of our professionals
- The *skills* that we need
- The *knowledge* and information we use
- The *reputation* of we firm—often an important determinant of the impact that our services have

Within our firm, the value base is used to "produce" services through a process of *value creation* that requires a number of critical process functions to deliver a successful service:

- *A strong vision and strategy that specify what our goals are and how we want to ach*ieve *them.*
- The *organization* that is defined by its structure and processes.
- The unwritten but very influential *culture* of our firm.
- Our *earnings model* that describes how we earn our fees and pay our people.

Finally, the value is delivered. This *value delivery* takes place:

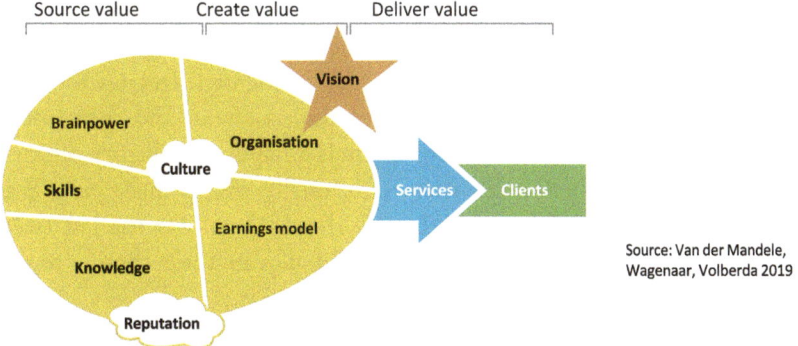

Fig. 2.6 A business model for the professional service firm

- *Through services that w*e perform.
- To *clients* who enjoy the benefits of our work.

The following diagram illustrates our business model (see Fig. 2.6):

2.6 How We Work Today: Our Archetypes and Their Limitations

Professional firms come in many flavors and colors. From the solitary village lawyer to the impressive big four accountants in the metropolis cities. From small-scale family law to corporate accounts. From one-to-one counseling to change processes with 100+ project workers. It pays to look at the different varieties—archetypes—of professional firms and see how they react to disruptions which we have discussed.[7]

2.6.1 Our Gentlemen's Club

Traditionally, our firm in the legal profession, accounting, or consulting is a *gentlemen's club* in which the partners are owner and manager and feel that way. Every partner is also master of his own practice with juniors who

[7] Kirkpatrick and Ackroyd (2003).

are learning the trade from him. Traditionally every partner earns the same—lock-step—often with an adjustment for years of service.[8] A classic image from past times: a couple of older gentlemen, feet on the table, loudly debating the profit allocation of the past year, and the associate who may join their club next year. There is an apocryphal story of one of the top law firms in Europe who traditionally would meet New Year's morning to determine how much they should earn over the last twelve months and subsequently how they should allocate these charges to each of their clients.

Initially our gentlemen's club is controlled by its founders, but after the first few years of growth a collegial partnership usually takes over in which major decisions are taken jointly by the partners. If the partnership exceeds 6–10 people, it is usually decided to allocate topics to committees in which a few members of the partnership take on a responsibility—such as recruitment or marketing. That goes well until the firm exceeds 20–30 partners and management work becomes too much work for a partner who is much more interested in his own professional work. A few partners are then asked to devote themselves to the daily management for a limited time, with which the partnership for the first time delegates important responsibilities. In most instances, the ensuing executive board is appointed for such a short period that it does not have much power to really change things. The gentlemen's club at this stage is culture driven, with few written rules and a lot of unwritten norms. For young people and colleagues, it is important to participate in this culture, which is usually not conducive to change.

---

[8] Greenwood and Empson (2003).

The gentlemen's club excels in giving partners the opportunity to exploit their individual skills and their talents with the support and leverage of a team of juniors. This makes this business model ideally suited for services that require individual qualities, such as external expertise and coaching. The dominance of the partners and interest of the group sometimes makes it more difficult for juniors to be creative and innovative.

The partners in the gentlemen's club are the boss, and when making strategic decisions they usually keep a close eye on their own interests. Many of them are less interested in rapid strategic change and large investments. Therefore, these firms often struggle with the ICT revolution and NewGen employees who have a different life- and work style, and do not fit the pattern. The model of the gentlemen's club becomes increasingly less effective with a larger size and with greater geographical and functional complexity. It also is very difficult for a gentleman's club to make acquisitions and form alliances.

For the scale needed for globalization gentlemen's club traditionally has two options—growing into a corporation or set up alliances with (foreign) firms. After all, the club is a form of democracy and has its own unique ways of doing[9].…

---

[9] Christensen et al. (2013).

2.6.2 The Professional Corporation

Many firms that grow gradually migrate to a hierarchically arranged *professional corporation*.[10] This in particular was the case in the second half of the last century when companies became larger and the world smaller thanks to telephone and airplane and there was a demand for scale and internationalization. With the growth came the need for more management and the professionalism. Famous names? DLA Piper and Baker McKenzie in the legal profession and McKinsey and BCG in consultancy (although they like to see themselves as partnerships). And the big four (PWC, Deloitte, EY, and KPMG) in accountancy.[11] Some, such as Accenture, even have gone far as to obtain a listing on the stock market and, like every listed company, set up a management structure with external supervisory directors. In the corporation, partners de facto work in a hierarchy albeit that they usually also are the shareholders who have indirect influence on appointments and policy. For the remainder these firms are managed top-down. Sometimes the firm will even opt for a shareholder structure—PLC or GmbH in Germany which legally calls for public oversight.

The corporate firm is particularly suited for large projects that require leadership and connections and for which expertise has to be sourced from across borders. Corporate firms have the resources to make large investments and can therefore lead the way with new information and communication systems as well as comprehensive training programs. They also have the financial means to sign off on major and risk-sharing contracts, which positions them well in a time when clients want their professionals to participate in the results of their project. Because large corporate firms can guarantee a certain quality and performance over their entire network, they are a logical partner for clients that globalize. This potential, however, (literally) has a price: corporate firms have high overhead costs and therefore need high fees. And creative professionals tend to feel less at home in a more hierarchical structure.[12] That is why clients also look for more economic solutions, for example by calling on local firms for local work or by deploying professional freelancers.

---

[10] Pinnington and Morris (2003), Cooper et al. (1996), Rao and Kenney (2008).
[11] Suddaby and Greenwood (2006).
[12] Malhotra et al. (2010).

Consequently, KPMG decided in 2015 to split off their small business practice in the Netherlands under the name "216 accountants" and sold their ownership to a private equity investor. Three years later, the new firm has grown to three branches and just announced its first acquisition of Ceifer Accountants, a specialist in the medical sector.

The professional hierarchy. Is this our future?

Management is going out of fashion

It appears that management is quickly losing popularity. The job of manager is not taken for granted any more. As ongoing efficiency measures grip many organizations, hierarchical layers are stripped, and management functions disappear. But is not only the drive toward cost reduction and simplification that is behind this change. It also seems that the value added of management, once beyond doubt, is disappearing.

The Peter Principle: how making a career means becoming a manager

Many people have gone through a personal drama in their working life which Professor Peter so well catches with his Principle: "In a hierarchy every employee tends to rise to his level of incompetence." Being good in their job, they are promoted and promoted again until they reach a level where they find they no longer perform. Many good people are invited into management positions for which they were not trained nor experienced. A recipe for failure in a successful career! Business schools flourish with their offerings for leadership training in professional services.

(continued)

(continued)
Sometimes this helps: not all formerly excellent craftsmen are unhappy with their new role. And in some cases, natural talents for management find new added value in their new jobs. But many fail, or at least are unhappy, until an eventual return to their original profession provides them relief. The question at hand is whether promotion to a management position would be still the inevitable way forward. Somebody has to do the job! Let's have a look at the appreciation of management as such.

Societal and technical developments change the nature of management
The definition of many management positions has changed dramatically over the past few decades. Some of the most relevant developments:

- Employees on average have a much better education and are therefore better equipped to perform their tasks independently. There is less need for direct instruction and supervision.
- Simple jobs are disappearing through a range of information technologies. This wipes out a lot of unskilled work. And we nowadays also offshore a good amount of this work.
- Today, information is ubiquitous and access to knowledge is easy. As a result, a lot of the coordinative work that management does that was based on the limited availability of information is disappearing.
- In our super-competitive world companies seek to eliminate any activity that does not add immediate value. Cutting overhead is a favorite. Companies are tempted to scrap management positions and then see what the consequences are.
- New generations are differently raised and much less boss dependent than their predecessors.
- The trend toward network organizations and "chains" at least ask for different coordinative roles and make classical management more or less obsolete.

This list is not exhaustive. In reaction, new approaches have been introduced to lead, plan, and control organizations. More and more organizations are relying on trust, self-management, and the natural motivation of most employees instead of costly management.

This requires alignment of vision about the company and its mission, an emphasis of values, full sharing of information and knowledge, and ample freedom to act—within clear boundaries. Social control and new attitudes toward work—more empowered and responsible—are other mechanisms that permit organizations to operate with a minimum of management.

Back to craftsmanship and professional excellence
What is happening in modern management theory is quite applicable to our firms. Back to the professions and professional work instead of supervising and controlling. Do you master a professional field? Hope so!

2.6.3 The Flexfirm

Flexwork has become increasingly popular in recent years. In the USA, for example, 30 percent of workers have a flex contract, working in the so-called gig economy.[13, 14] These flex workers are often associated with *flexfirms* that offer job brokerage in the legal, accounting, and consulting world, usually supported by central account management, training, and specialist functions. Recruits are often professionals who come from established firms and who want to work part-time for private reasons, with flexible working hours. Some firms have layers of flex workers with different levels of commitment and loyalty. Eden McCallum is a good example of a flexfirm in consultancy. USG in accountancy and Axiom, Omnius, and LeanLawyer are a few of the many names in the legal profession. Marjon Wanders of Eden McCallum consultants explains:

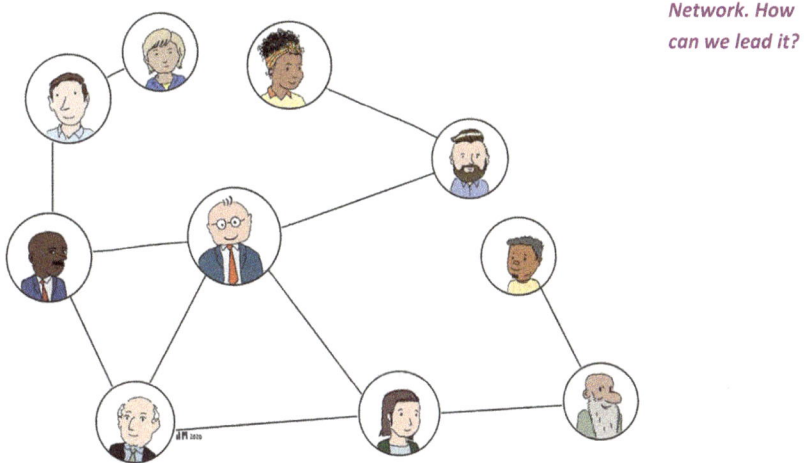

Network. How can we lead it?

"Clients like to work with us because we are flexible for our employees and creative for our clients, with lower rates than international consultancies. We only have limited own research although we have started recruiting a small team of analysts. We however hardly find that a disadvantage

---

[13] Powell (1990).
[14] Mckinsey Global Institute (2016).

anymore because in this information age almost everything can be found on-line."

Flexfirms may well be effective in providing many professional functions such as expertise, interim management, and training and coaching. Flexfirms may also respond well to the demands of NewGen professionals. But flexfirms usually do not have the resources to invest in ambitious tech-related projects, while the difficulty of dealing effectively with global and complex assignments can also be a problem for them. This explains why many firms have opted for a loose form of the flexfirm: the *alliance*.

An alliance usually only has central coordination and may permit its members to work with outside competitors.[15] The alliance is still a popular form to gain access to different disciplines or markets without much investment. In law a good example of a relatively tight alliance is the best friends structure between the white shoe firms of Slaughter and May in London, Bredin Prat in Paris, Hengeler Mueller in Frankfurt, Uría Menéndez in Madrid, and De Brauw in Amsterdam—each top rated in their own market. Between them, they make joint investments in new markets (e.g., China) and new activities (e.g., artificial intelligence). With best friends there is a strong pressure to cross-refer, but no obligation. Most other alliances in law (e.g., Lex Mundi, the World Law Group, or InterLaw) and accounting have a much more loose and non-committal structure. As such they start to look like the ecosystems that we know for example from the electronics and fashion industries, in which companies share and compete at the same time.[16] In professional services, most alliances either bond together into professional corporations or stagnate as relatively loose confederations.[17] The alliance, however, can be an effective way to temporarily meet the challenge of globalization with only modest investment.

An alternative hierarchical structure that clients can opt for are in-house professional services—the internal audit service, the corporate lawyer, and the internal advisory service. They have been on the rise in recent years because they of course have intimate knowledge of their (dedicated) company, and because they usually have more modest remuneration

---

[15] Moore (1993).
[16] Nohria and Eccles (1992).
[17] Salvoldi and Brock (2019).

packages than independent lawyers. They are reputed not to attract the most innovative and aggressive staff.

Many client companies face a difficult strategic choice in keeping professional staff departments in-house, or outsourcing these functions.[18]

2.7 Today's Archetypes Are Not Sustainable

Each of these archetypes has its own strong sides. For example, the flexfirm can be a valuable playground for creative and talented professionals with a low-cost base that may give it a strong competitive position against the traditional gentlemen's club. The latter will rely more on its experienced seniors and their strong coach–apprentice links, supported by a strong culture. Corporate firms have the resources and broad networks to provide a full range of skills and knowledge with global reach. Each of the archetypes is seriously challenged by the four disruptions that are underway:

- The demands of the new generations pose difficult recruitment and retention problems in particular for the traditional gentleman's club and corporate firms.
- New technologies are having a dramatic impact on the way knowledge is managed in the professional world and the skills that are needed to work with these technologies. This involves major change and investment, which are hurdles for gentleman's clubs and flexfirms.
- The increasing complexity of the problems that clients pose will also make life difficult for gentleman's clubs and flexfirms.
- And finally, the relentless drive of clients to more value at lower cost means that the corporate firms increasingly find themselves on the losing side of competition.

The following diagram shows how all these disruptions in our environment affect the elements of the model of our professional service firm (see Fig. 2.7).

---

[18] Coase (1937), Williamson (1981).

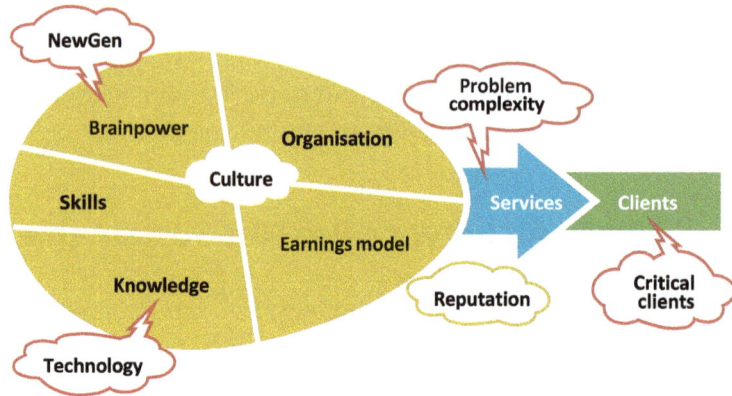

Fig. 2.7 Disruption of our business

In this environment, the traditional gentlemen's club thrives less well. The route to partnership with the associated reputation and rewards takes too much time. The hard work required in the intervening years leaves little for leisure and private pursuits. In addition, the adjustments within the firm for new technologies and globalization cost a lot of money and time. Not every partner is willing to make that investment.[19] The corporation nowadays has too much hierarchy and less entrepreneurship and not enough recognition for the individual contribution. Access to capital and international networks is less a problem, access to the best (junior) professionals all the more.

But the model ends up being quite rigid and usually does not leave enough latitude for entrepreneurship and innovation. Also the cost structure leads to very high fees, which is not acceptable for many clients. The flexfirm meets the concerns of younger generations but threatens to shift the balance too far on the other side. Many flexfirms consist of individuals with little team interaction. Investments and training in competencies, knowledge, and IT are mostly left to the participant and therefore are underinvested. Work in flexfirms can be lonely, which explains that many people find this attractive only for a number of years, for example, if a family is started, or as a bridge to

---

[19] Malhotra et al. (2010).

one's own—independent—company, or in the latter stage of their career. In the long term, many flexfirmers end up preferring permanent employment.

2.7.1 Which Model Is the Most Forward-Looking?

If we look forward to the challenges of the future, we see two priorities come to the fore. Firstly, we must make sure that the ongoing business continues to pay; current practice must be exploited to support the continuity of our operation in the immediate term and to generate funds for the investments that we must do in the future.[20] Secondly: we want to explore new avenues for the future.

We have clouds – but also a silver lining

---

[20] Ilinitch et al. (1996), March (1991), Volberda (1996).

Exploitation means providing existing services to our clients and realizing a good price so that we can earn decent revenues. For this, we need professionals who have a sense of efficiency and can leverage larger teams of juniors and resources so we can limit the unit cost of our services with as little risk as possible. If we watch the archetypes mentioned above, we see that the professional corporation is an excellent model for large corporations and complex tasks. Of course, it is also appropriate in these practices to maximize the use of software, which is often effective and low cost especially in routine tasks. Furthermore, investments in professional service products paid for by the largest clients can later be sold to medium/small clients at a low sales price—a process known as the "Robin Hood" principle.[21] This is also a suitable environment for the IT-driven firms that start with major investment in software and data development that then is "exploited." To explore new ways (exploration), we need creative entrepreneurs who seek new paths and are willing to take risks. These innovators want freedom and flexibility that we can accommodate very well in a flexfirm.[22]

But what do we do if we want to be a firm that simultaneously exploits our ongoing practices and also explores new roads, in a two-sided (in jargon: ambidextrous) organization? The solution can then be found in a division of exploitation and exploration into different departments or even locations. Experience shows that integrating the two functions of exploiting today and exploring the future in one organization almost always requires too much of the culture of our organization. Nonetheless, many firms try to keep the exploration of new activities and the exploitation of the existing within their own team as the dynamics of the market and competitive pressures increase. This can be referred to as "contextual ambiguity"[23]: individual consultants, accountants, and lawyers are motivated through incentives and a supporting culture to be even more efficient in providing ongoing services, while also being continuously challenged to develop new activities. The latter usually in vain because the pressure from clients and competitors combined with the need to earn one's bonus/fee within the trusted earnings model gives no opportunity, time, and resources to explore new avenues. That is why most explorative

---

[21] Van den Bosch et al. (2005).
[22] Tushman and O'Reilly (1996), Volberda (1998).
[23] Abell (1993), Gibson and Birkinshaw (2004), Bervort and Suddaby (2016).

2 Understanding How Professionals Work: Building Blocks… 59

initiatives end in a spin-off (and an alliance with the old company). A striking example of this development is McKinsey Solutions, a firm that uses artificial intelligence and big data analysis for strategy development.

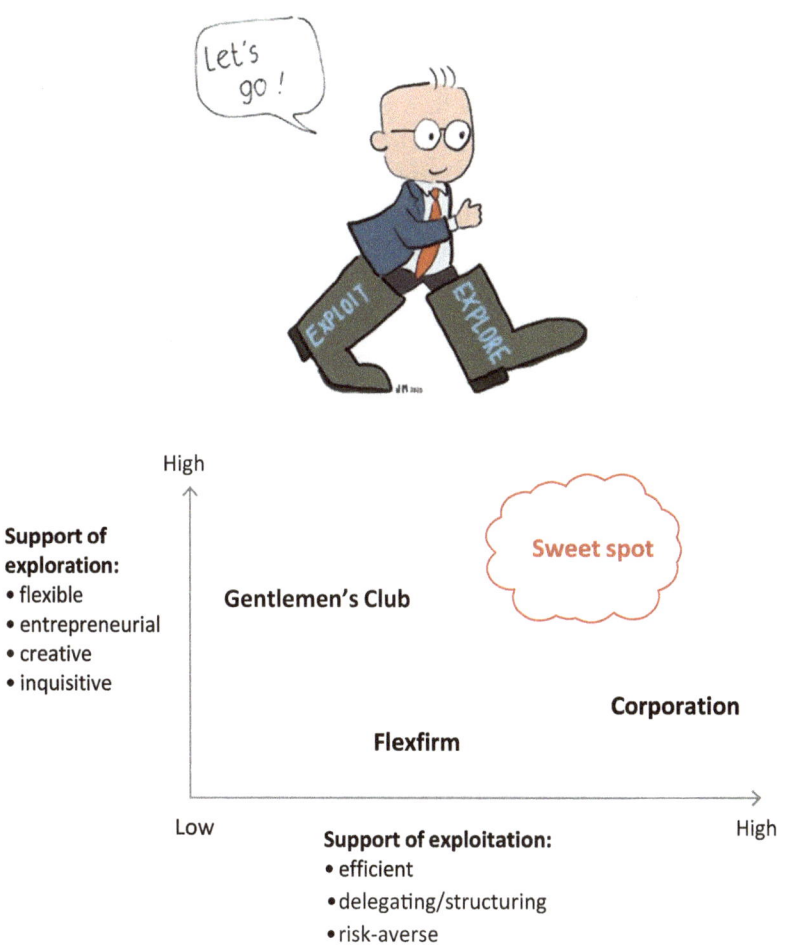

Fig. 2.8 Exploration and exploitation by archetypes

If we project the exploitation of our traditional and familiar business model on one axis in a diagram and the need to explore new businesses on the other, we can plot the various archetypes (see Fig. 2.8).

We also see that there is a "sweet spot," an archetype that would make it possible to both exploit and explore. That sweet spot exists, we shall see, in the form of a professional community.[24]

Most major international professional corporations recognize the dilemma. As the managing partner of a top European law firm expressed it: "Work for the top of the market requires creativity and therefore autonomous lawyers. When a firm grows, it starts to look like a normal company which is deadly for creativity. Internationally, we work together with other firms in a network and therefore have a better proposition. If our foreign friends do not deliver enough quality, we can always switch." A German senior partner of one multi-service firm gives his perspective on the challenge:

"In our group we have become a large multinational with a variety of practices. But my consultancy department defines quality differently from the other units. For us quality mainly depends on a good selection of people, on the exemplary role of seniors, and on training. The rates of our consulting department are three times higher than the average of our global firm. We tend to look at rates and contract prices but most of our colleagues look mainly at costs and capacity utilization which is not interesting for us. But our colleagues appreciate us because we generate sales for them. The staff departments hold the firm together and drive it ahead globally. But they also are dogmatic and inflexible."

We can contrast this with the remarks by the partner of a small expert group Merlin (to be discussed in more detail in the next chapter) who says: "I am totally flexible with almost zero overheads. When I need more geographic or functional scope, I turn to my friends at BCG—the Boston Consulting Group—with whom I have an excellent cooperative arrangement." As we discussed before, Slaughter and May has tried to solve the problem by creating a "best friends" alliance with six top European firms to take cooperation a step further: "With our best friends we can adapt to customer needs and provide a single point of contact and one bill," says the Managing Partner of its Amsterdam branch.

The search is on for a new model that on the one hand uses the new technological means effectively and at the lowest cost to the client and on

---

[24] March (1991), Mom et al. (2009), Bevort and Suddaby (2016).

the other hand offers its own employees a motivating job with entrepreneurship and flexibility. How do we piece together a way of working that effectively and efficiently accommodates a variety of different and complementary capabilities. And with which colleagues also do we feel a "click." How do we do it?

If we want our professional firms to exist and succeed 5–10 years from now, we should get started immediately with a redesign. The changes taking place around us are too fundamental and too threatening. Traditional solutions—saving costs, a new software package, an alliance—are useful but do not suffice. Continuing in the same way therefore is an option that will ultimately be fatal. Precisely because business is so good at the moment we hesitate to move. Fortunately, we have a business model available that does meet the new requirements of clients and professionals, and is made possible by the new information and communication technologies: *the professional community*.

References

Abell, D. F. (1993). *Managing with dual strategies*. Free Press.
Bevort, F., & Suddaby, R. (2016). Scripting professional identities: How individuals make sense of contradictory logics. *Journal of Professions and Organization, 3*(1), 17–38.
Christensen, C. M., Wang, D., & Van Bever, D. (2013). Consulting in the Cusp of disruption. *Harvard Business Review, 91*(10), 106–114.
Coase, R. (1937). The nature of the firm. *Economica, 4*(16), 386–405.
Cooper, D. J., Hinings, C. R., Greenwood, R., & Brown, J. (1996). Sedimentation and transformation in organizational change: The case of Canadian law firms. *Organization Studies, 17*(4), 623–647.
Gibson, C. B., & Birkinshaw, J. (2004). The antecedents, consequences, and mediating role of organizational ambidexterity. *Academy of Management Journal, 47*(2), 209–226.
Greenwood, R., & Empson, L. (2003). The professional partnership: Relic or exemplary form of governance? *Organization Studies, 24*(6), 909–934.
Ilinitch, A. Y., D'Aveni, R., & Lewin, A. (1996). New organization forms and strategies for managing in hypercompetitive environments. *Organization Science, 7*(3), 211–220.

Kirkpatrick, I., & Ackroyd, S. (2003). Archetype theory and the changing professional organisation: A critique and alternative. *Organization, 10*(4), 731–750.

Maister, D. H., Green, C. H., & Galford, R. M. (2000). *The trusted advisor.* Free Press.

Malhotra, N., Morris, T., & Smets, M. (2010). New career models in UK professional service firms: From up-or-out to up-and-going-nowhere? *The International Journal of Human Resource Management, 21*(9), 1396–1413.

March, J. G. (1991). Exploration and exploitation in organizational learning. *Organization Science, 2*, 71–87.

McKinsey Global Institute. (2016). *Choice, necessity and the Gig economy.* McKinsey & Company.

Mom, T. J. M., Van den Bosch, F. A. J., & Volberda, H. W. (2009). Understanding variation in manager's ambidexterity: Investigating direct and indirect interaction effects of formal structural and personal coordination mechanisms. *Organization Science, 20*(4), 812–828.

Moore, J. F. (1993). Predators and prey: A new ecology of competition. *Harvard Business Review, 71*(3), 75–86.

Nohria, N., & Eccles, R. G. (1992). *Networks and organizations: Structure, form and action.* Harvard Business School Press.

Osterwalder, A., & Pigneur, Y. (2010). *Business model generation.* Wiley.

Pinnington, A. H., & Morris, T. (2003). Archetype change in professional organizations: Survey evidence from large law firms. *British Journal of Management, 14*(1), 85–99.

Powell, W. P. (1990). Neither market nor hierarchy: Network forms of organization. *Research for Organizational Behaviour, 12*, 295–336.

Rao, H., & Kenney, M. (2008). New forms as settlements. In R. Greenwood, C. Oliver, K. Sahlin, & R. Suddaby (Eds.), *The sage handbook of organizational institutionalism* (1st ed., pp. 352–370). Sage.

Salvoldi, R., & Brock, D. M. (2019). Opening the black box of psf network internationalization: An exploration of law firm networks. *Journal of Professions and Organization, 6*(3), 304–322.

Suddaby, R., & Greenwood, R. (2006). Institutional entrepreneurship in mature fields: The big five accounting firms. *Academy of Management Journal, 49*(1), 27–48.

Tushman, M. L., & O'Reilly, C. A. (1996). Ambidextrous organizations: Managing evolutionary and revolutionary change. *California Management Review, 38*, 8–30.

Van den Bosch, F. A. J., Baaij, M. G., & Volberda, H. W. (2005). How knowledge accumulation has changed strategy consulting: Strategic options for established strategy consulting. *Strategic Change, 14*(1), 25–34.

Van der Mandele, H.C. (2006) *Economic apoptosis and uncontrollability, a first enquiry into the concepts and their relevance for the market-government debate*, Diss., University of Groningen.

Van der Mandele, L. M., & Parker, J. M. (2009). *Changing the Leopard's spots. Renewal of the professional firm*. Pearson Education.

Van der Mandele, L. M., Volberda, H. W. & Wagenaar, R. (2019). *De nieuwe professional service firm: Hoe advocaten, accountants & adviseurs zichzelf opnieuw uitvinden*, Scriptum Publishers.

Volberda, H. W. (1996). Toward the flexible form: How to remain vital in hypercompetitive environments. *Organization Science, 7*(4), 359–372.

Volberda, H. W. (1998). *Building the flexible firm: How to remain competitive*. Oxford University Press.

Volberda, H. W., Van den Bosch, F. A. J., & Heij, K. (2018). *Reinventing business models, how firms cope with disruption*. Oxford University Press.

Williamson, O. E. (1981). The economics of organization: The transaction cost approach. *The American Journal of Sociology, 87*(3), 548–577.

3

Profiting from Disruption

3.1 Introducing Case Studies on Business Communities

The professional services are a very dynamic arena that offers great opportunities for entrepreneurship and innovation. It is not surprising to see ventures emerging that capitalize on the new technologies and offer opportunities for new generations who want to avoid what they see as the treadmill to partnership.[1] The following pages contain short case descriptions of firms that have developed into professional communities, or at least have learning points for professional communities. Some of these, such as Merlin, are one-man shows with a narrow scope—in this instance limited to expert opinion on telecommunications licenses. Some others, such as the Berkeley Research Group (BRG), have hundreds of associated professionals and cover a range of professional services with office locations across the globe. The Bureau for Software Development (BSO) is a special case, being a network of more or less independent software companies with thousands of employees. These cases show that you no longer have to follow traditional structures in order to succeed in professional services.[2]

---

[1] Broderick (2011).
[2] Fiol and Romenelli (2012).

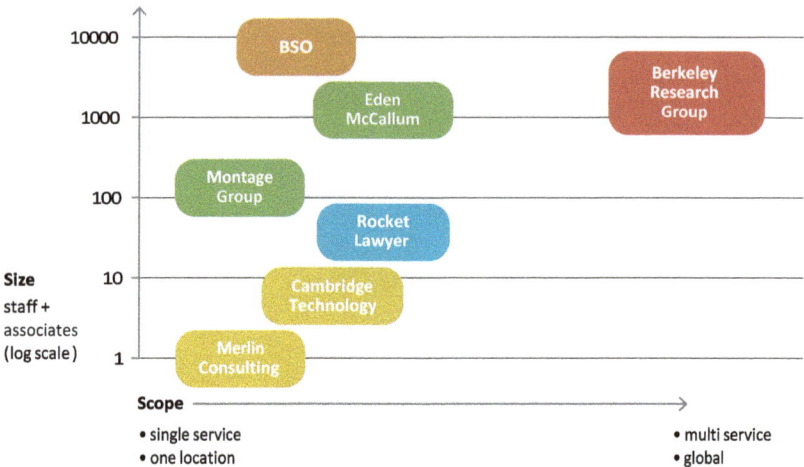

Fig. 3.1 Size and scope of professional communities

Below, we first describe two small expert firms—Merlin and Cambridge Technology Consulting Group (CTCG)—and then go into the larger operations of Montage Group and Eden McCallum. Rocket Lawyer warrants its own review as a software-based provider of legal services. Finally, we discuss the Berkeley Research Group as an example of a fully-fledged and functioning professional community. As we can see below, the cases differ substantially in size and the scope of their activities (see Fig. 3.1).

3.2 Two Expert Communities: Cambridge Technology and Merlin

Jerold Savin and seven "best friends" formed the *Cambridge Technology Consulting Group (CTCG)*, a community that provides IT guidance to medium-sized ($50 mln to 1 bln revenue) businesses, including software selection and implementation, data architecture design, litigation support, interim management, training, and coaching, to list a few of their activities.

"Most of us are based in Southern California, but we do not meet very often and there are members that I have worked with for seven years without ever seeing them. We are very selective in who we admit to our group, and through the years we have come to fully trust the quality of each other's work, even if people work remotely. On average we spend about 50% of our time working on CTCG projects, the remainder on individual non-related projects," says Jerold.

Modern Merlin – a bit of IT and a lot of wisdom

"Our selling propositions are software management expertise and excellent personal client relationship. Each of us does his own selling, selects his team members and manages his case. Being a consultancy without overheads, we deliver excellent value for money—a high level of insight for a very low price. In my experience, physical contact is essential for good client relations in the kind of managerial projects in which we are involved, which explains why most of our practice is located in Southern California. We are very happy with our strategic position as it is. Growth is not easy: finding and incorporating new members is a challenge. Because of our size, we have an uneven deal flow and find that adding new clients is not easy. Large firms benefit from their brand and resources, which enable them to invest heavily in marketing and account management. Their market "gravitas" (reputation and credibility) supports the sometimes ridiculously high prices that they charge. To cite an example: we recently offered a training job to Disney for $30,000, which was subsequently given to one of the big three strategy houses for one million dollars!"

Communications technology strategist Malcolm Ross about his consultancy, *Merlin*: "Merlin is a single-person office built into a worldwide expert network—a weak form of community—in the field of bandwidth licenses for telecom companies. Clients span the globe and include Vodafone and Deutsche Telekom. I do my own selling and account management and spend a lot of time on networking with clients and prospects. I work with a group of professionals that I trust. Most of them are small outfits, such as Auction Technologies, who have around six semi-independent experts on contracting, including lawyers. But when needed, I can also call on BCG—the Boston Consulting Group, where I know the relevant partners well. It then becomes a superior way to manage even large projects, even if it does not have a single brand and leadership. Our keys to network success are alignment (culture) and motivation ("hungry artists"). I like to compare us with a film production company where 500+ people spend a lot of money within the average of 42 days required for the shooting. Or a symphony orchestra."

3.3 Flexible Consulting and Law: Eden McCallum and the Montage Legal Group

"It takes no effort at all for us to find the best consultants," says Liann Eden, founding partner of *Eden McCallum LLP* in London.

"The majority of our people are alumni of "MBB"—McKinsey, BCG or Bain—with more than two years of experience. But we also receive many excellent candidates from firms that have been taken over, such as Booz and Monitor. What they are looking for is freedom. Freedom to choose when they want to get started and what assignment they want to carry out. Freedom to go away for a few months with impunity, to spend time on family or a hobby. Our people are experts in their field.

Our clients appreciate their competencies, maturity and entrepreneurship. We do not have the usual pyramid, but almost only experienced consultants and experts. We keep up our skills with monthly training sessions and intensive on-the-job coaching. In addition, it helps that we have small teams. Most of our jobs are with operational units—divisions and business units—and we are less well-equipped to mobilize large teams. We are happy to leave that work to our colleagues at the major international strategy houses. They in turn are not always inclined to deploy their large and expensive teams for somewhat smaller and time-fragmented projects. We have an excellent synergy with these firms."

Marjon Wanders, senior partner and founder of the Amsterdam office, adds: "Our consultants have a reputation for being totally familiar with the industry and functioning of their client. Our clients do not have the patience to work with inexperienced professionals. And we can listen very well and have no preconceptions about what is good for the client and what is not. We are flexible, creative, good at working in mixed teams and in co-creation. And we are flexible: if a client makes an unexpected request or a job may be delayed, this is no problem for us. And because we have little overhead, our rates are lower than those of the corporate firms. The result is good." Eden McCallum was founded in 2000 and now has a team of more than 500 consultants available, of whom more than 100 are working continuously and the others part-time. The firm now has three locations—London, Amsterdam, and Zurich.

Liann: "What we find challenging compared to our corporate competitors? Large investments in recruitment and development of people who are not profitable for a longer period of time, with an increased risk of failure, are more difficult for us. This makes it difficult to start up new branches across borders, for example. And that also applies to new information technologies. Therefore, we do have a number of analysts on the staff who support us with big data analysis and internet searches.

Professional with a balanced life – usually!

Information and knowledge development are areas we focus on." In most respects, Eden McCallum is a very successful community. But there is no structure to team up experts in the same area into industrial or functional practices—which a fully-fledged community such as BRG does have.

The leaders of the *Montage Group*, Laurie Rowans and Erin Giglia, look like two high-flying professional lawyers from a white shoe firm in New York or Washington. Nothing indicates that they are founder/owners of the most successful employment agency for lawyers on the US West Coast. In California, the prestigious title these days is "founder," and they carry this title with pride. Montage was founded in 2008 in Laurie's living room and has since experienced continuous growth. The company now has more than 200 lawyers on its list.

Both founders started their career as lawyers at a large firm in Los Angeles. They broke off their careers because they wanted a more flexible agenda. Today, many women and men at the large firms are looking for the same flexibility in their working year, working week, and working day. Montage Group receives calls from medium and small local law firms when they experience surges in demand or when they need part-time specialist expertise. The emphasis was and is on firms in Southern California. According to Laurie and Erin, the starting point for Montage's success is the careful selection of lawyers who, without exception, have worked for a number of years for one of the top firms in Southern

California. Finding new lawyers is no problem: Montage has an excellent reputation and enough lawyers seem to be interested in a flexible job.

3.3.1 Flexible Job: With Quality Results!

Most of the lawyers at Montage are women, who in this way can combine their work with their family life. Sometimes people join out of interest in the content of the work and for reasons of ambition, but financial considerations also play a role. Among the male participants in Montage, time for the family and the desire to take long vacations, to pursue a time-consuming hobby, or to start a new career are also arguments. Most lawyers work five or six years for Montage, and then return to a full-time job at a law firm. That also explains why Montage does limited training. Some people make arrangements themselves, while many others are less concerned. Montage's unique selling is the personal attention that it pays to its clients and lawyers through regular personal contact. Montage has weekly telephone talks with its lawyers and also regularly organizes "family meetings" to keep up with legal and social issues. These are mostly conducted by phone and always with an open ear for the personal and business circumstances of both the client and the lawyer. Contact sessions are at least once a month and more frequent at the beginning and the end of a project.

This enables quality to be monitored. In the few instances when things go wrong, Montage offers a replacement for free. The lawyer with substandard performance usually gets a second chance with another client, but rarely a third. The same applies to unreasonable or unethical clients.

New clients seek out Montage because they are aware of its reputation. But the website also plays an important role. As mentioned, most clients are medium-sized and small law firms, but legal departments of corporations account for a fifth of turnover. The past few years have seen an increase in the number of clients from outside Southern California. They are now not only based throughout California but also across the entire USA, with affiliated freelancers in major urban areas such as New York, Boston, Chicago, and Washington, DC. Montage is growing steadily and has never had a revenue downturn—not even during the 2009–2010 recession or the COVID-19 crisis of 2020. The company now has 250 lawyers on its list of freelancers, to which a maximum of five names are added each month. Montage receives dozens of applications per month and can therefore be very selective. Of those 250 names, approximately 100 FTEs are working for Montage at any given time. One recent project was the recruitment of an administrative staff member and the introduction of a CRM program to keep track of all the lawyers. Montage's profit margins are solid.

Somewhat to Laurie and Erin's surprise, their approach may also be working over longer distances. Clients often call after having heard about Montage from a Californian colleague or after having visited the website. Communication with more remote clients and lawyers is by phone and e-mail, but also using Skype and WhatsApp, which appear to be a reasonable alternative to personal contact. This also applies to the application process that has to be meticulous if only because central controls are limited. Montage thus feels that it is important for its people to regularly meet in person and there have been several attempts to appoint regional representatives to take charge in other regions—so far without success.

Montage faces a number of strategic decisions for the near future. First, there is the question of how to expand further. Should the emphasis remain on California, or should investments be made on the East Coast or in cities such as Seattle and Chicago? Closely related is the question of Erin and Laurie's increasing workload. To date, the experience with local representatives in the Midwest has not been very good, but perhaps this was due to a lack of critical selection and training. It appears to be difficult to find colleagues who pay the same attention to personal relationships and quality. A second important question is how to deal with AI and big data programs, which are being introduced everywhere. Montage has discussed this with a number of information-driven law services providers, such as Rocket Lawyer. At the same time, it appears that many of the affiliated lawyers have their own software and databases, so it is not certain whether Montage should become involved in AI and big data programs. Finally, there is a private equity investor who wants to take a stake in the company, which would greatly increase its financial clout. But it is less clear what should be done with this capital. After all, the core business is people-intensive, not capital-intensive. Laurie and Erin value their independence. They are convinced that their emphasis on personal contact with clients and lawyers, and the insight it gives them into the needs and abilities of both groups, is the secret of their success.

3.4 Computer-Based Professional Services: Rocket Lawyer

Rocket Lawyer was founded in 2008 to provide computer-based legal services to consumer and small business markets. Rocket Lawyer combines a vast database of contract and procedure examples with intelligent (AI) software to guide the client to the right document. As founder/CEO Charley Moore indicates: "Law is incredibly expensive at this moment and most people cannot afford decent contracts. Rocket Lawyer makes law affordable by producing computer formulated contracts and opinions. Consumers can now write agreements with their plumber and gardener instead of trusting a handshake. We have a patent on generating cloud documents with the assistance of a licensed lawyer. Rocket Lawyer and its competitors open a huge new market and do not reduce the workload of traditional law firms." Rocket Lawyer carefully selects its supporting lawyers, provides them with entry training, and keeps track of their performance.

It has also signed contracts with 250 corporate clients, such as Google and Amazon, who offer Rocket Lawyer subscriptions to their employees. The company now has 200 full-time employees and many more part-timers. Startups in Spain, France, and the Netherlands are part of a growth strategy aimed at going global, including in developing countries.[3]

---

[3] Armour and Sako (2020).

3.5 A Community of Software Firms: BSO/Bureau for Software Development

A source of inspiration for the professional service community is the Bureau for Software Development (BSO), which was founded by Eckart Wintzen in 1976 and was a rapidly growing success for more than 15 years. This was thanks to its unique organizational approach. A merger with the software activities of Philips in 1990 resulted in a company with 10,000 employees and 75 offices in 20 countries. Shortly thereafter, the company was sold to ATOS (a French software multinational) and changed into a "normal," i.e., hierarchical company.

Henk Cohen, who succeeded Wintzen as CEO in 1994, summarizes it as follows: "BSO was a unique formula and a great success for many years. The company was divided into a large number of independent cells. These cells originally employed a maximum of 40 people and if they grew beyond that point, they were split into two or more cells. Because of the small size of the cells, there was little or no hierarchy, with very few controls and overheads, and the heads of cells could have intensive daily contact with all of their people. This was of course a great stimulus for entrepreneurship. The leader of each cell was expected to identify successors who could establish and lead the following cells.

Team competition...

The cells were controlled through "standards": annual targets for turnover, budget, quality and the like, whereby every cell was free to interpret these. Every quarter, the holding company measured the degree to which each cell met the standards. Incidentally, this also resulted in incidents in which a cell had luck with its bookings in the first month and then went on vacation to Japan for three weeks. This independence was far-reaching and included sales, hiring/firing and product development. And as BSO grew, there was increasing—and accepted—competition between the different cells. Cells were aware of each other's "standards" and competition was allowed. Capacity imbalances between cells were filled by the internal market. All this of course had a positive effect on entrepreneurship. Incidentally, major investments and innovations were kept outside the cell structure and paid for by the holding company.

For many years, the holding company was a minimalist set-up with a finance guy and no HR department.[4]

As BSO grew and expanded internationally, a number of flaws in the model emerged. There was little motivation for the cells to work together, which was a problem especially in working across borders. The cell structure also turned out to be unsuitable for large, complex projects where clients needed larger, centrally coordinated teams. As a result, cells became larger—up to 200 people or more—which in combination with the minimal central staff proved to function less well. With the acquisition of the software development division of Philips Electronics, BSO made the leap to a large multinational. The company subsequently lost control and profitability. BSO-Origin ended as part of the ATOS group and little is left of the unique original model and its wonderful, highly entrepreneurial and creative culture. My conclusion is that the model is still highly relevant, but that the definition and formulation of the standards should have evolved with the globalization of BSO's customers and organization, and the rapid development of IT technologies."

---

[4] Wintzen (2006).

3.6 The Berkeley Research Group: A Professional Community with a Wide Range of Services

BRG—the Berkeley Research Group—was founded in 2010 by David Teece, with a unique professional community model. Seven years later, BRG had three business lines:

- Disputes and investigation, which includes advice on damages, antitrust, class actions, and arbitration.
- Corporate finance, which includes investment banking and valuation.
- Strategy and operations, which includes strategy, business process improvement, and IT planning.

BRG – a great show with a terrific showmaster

BRG now employs 1100 professionals, who generate turnover of more than $400 million. How is BRG doing that, and what are the prospects and challenges of this success?

David Teece has been described as "the only one who is both a leading academic and a top manager." Originally from New Zealand, he studied business administration at the Wharton School of Finance and then became a professor at Stanford Business School. In 1982, he crossed San Francisco Bay to Berkeley University where he wrote more than a dozen books and 200 articles on strategy and policy. He was soon hired by companies to advise them on market organization, anti-cartel legislation, and competition issues, hiring staff and students to do the preparatory analytical work. That turned out to be an inefficient process because the composition of the team was constantly changing and he continually had to train new people. When he noticed that other professors at Berkeley had the same problem in their consultancy work, he and a number of colleagues decided to set up the Law and Economics Consulting Group (LECG) to strengthen their staff support. This group grew rapidly and prosperously, but made a number of strategic mistakes, as it turned out. Driven by the desire to expand rapidly, LECG quickly made a number of acquisitions and alliances. To finance this expansion, LECG brought in a private equity firm that quickly tightened the screws to boost returns. LECG got into trouble, and Teece followed a classic American success model by immediately establishing a new group with similar principles but without the previous mistakes.

3.6.1 A Unique Business Model

Teece originally decided to set up BRG as a professional community. At BRG the senior expert is central, and not the client as is customary in the mission statement of professional service firms. The senior expert is responsible for his own turnover, work, and income, and delivers an agreed gross margin (equals fees minus personal remuneration). He also takes care of recruiting juniors and developing knowledge and skills. BRG provides a number of supporting functions, such as marketing and brand, professional and administrative/IT support, and financing.

This approach reduces the administrative burden to a minimum. The community does not have to worry about a large number of processes, such as assessments, promotions, and bonus systems, which in most large professional organizations quickly become 30% or more of seniors' time. The consequence of this is that experts and management have considerably more time for clients and project work.

3 Profiting from Disruption   79

BRG's leadership primarily recruits, coaches, and monitors seniors—often entrepreneurial academics and similar experts. Clients are large corporations, banks, and law firms. The BRG partners are strongly focused on their clients and field of expertise, making them valuable to their clients and able to work very efficiently due to their experience. In this approach, the traditional junior who provides work support but also gives leverage to the income of the partners plays a much less important role. As a result, the BRG organization takes the form of a cylinder instead of a pyramid.

This approach has turned out to be lucrative: BRG, with sales per capita of more than $370,000, leaves most professional firms behind (see Fig. 3.2).

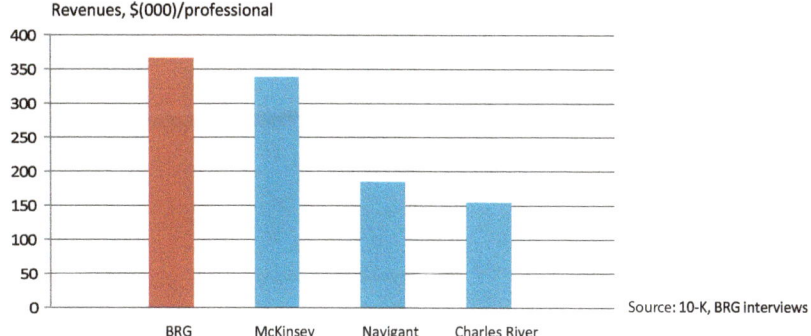

Fig. 3.2 Comparison of BRG with selected consultants

3.6.2 A Quick Start

BRG started in 2010 and has since grown by around 20% in both sales and staff every year. The unique strength of BRG is its ability to attract enterprising academics in a stimulating community that offers the necessary support for marketing and carrying out work, without the associated administrative burden. With BRG, the experts are able to charge high rates, most of which they can retain themselves. Moreover, the model is highly transparent. In this way, after seven years, turnover of more than $350 mln was achieved in 2017 (see Fig. 3.3).

BRG now has 23 offices spread across North and South America, Asia, and Europe.

To strengthen knowledge exchange and account management, BRG has formed teams (practice groups) of experts who deal with related clients and assignments. The supporting professional staff work in an internal market maintained by the office coordinators. The administration of the community is kept as light as possible.

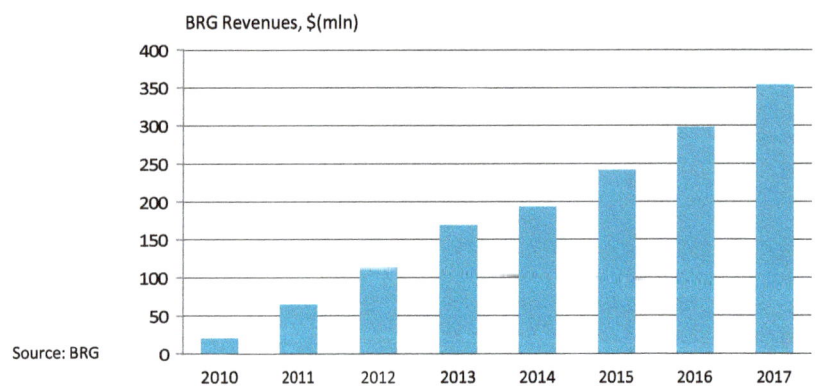

Fig. 3.3 BRG revenue growth 2010–2017

3.6.3 Challenges

Looking out of the window over the beautiful San Fransisco bay, Teece philosophizes: "I see the main challenges for BRG in maintaining the unique character of the group throughout its growth and strengthening its team culture. Experts are often individualists who are not particularly efficient and effective at inviting colleagues or juniors to join them in their work. According to the model, delegation *per se* is not a major problem because partners are responsible for their efficiency and delegation—or the lack of it. But the mutual sharing of knowledge and important clients and key accounts is a more substantive issue.

At BRG, we have established practice groups for this purpose. According to the BRG model, an expert is free to be a member of one or more practice groups—or, if desired, of none of them. Some of my senior colleagues argue for more mandatory participation in practice groups." In the short term, BRG notes that its loose community structure does not facilitate cost control. Every expert and every team wants its own office, which leads to a fragmentation of space and capacity. Every expert and every team has its own preferences with regard to software packages and IT systems, which leads to incremental expenses. At what point should the management impose its will? Even success has its challenges.

3.7 What We Have Learned from These Cases: Conclusions

These case stories show that new community-like ventures can be very successful in building on the disruptive changes of today. They all make very effective use of information and communications technologies—some, such as Merlin and Montage in a basic form, while others, such as Rocket Lawyer, use technology as the launch point for their business model. And they all capitalize on the need felt by many new-generation professionals for more flexibility in their careers as well as more freedom in their work schedules. It is with large, complex engagements that networked professionals fail and only a real professional community with its shared vision and trust between members succeeds. Of the cases listed, only BSO, Cambridge Technology, and BRG have these characteristics and the ability to succeed with complex work.

Cambridge Technology, though, has only ten members and is too small for large assignments. And BSO, as we have seen, made a number of strategic mistakes that led to its demise.

If we look at the prospects of success, we can see that focusing on a defined capability, clientele, or business model is important and a key driver of this success. Sometimes there is specific client base—as Rocket Lawyer and Merlin Consulting have. Sometimes an area of expertise is chosen—as with Montage or Cambridge Technology. And sometimes it is the business model itself—as with Berkeley Research Group and Eden McCallum. When these firms want to grow—and we have seen that growth is imperative—a modicum of control becomes important. The "associations of friends" of Merlin and Cambridge Technology rely heavily on their informal culture and have very limited formal controls, which limit the number of their participants to 10–20 members. Organizations such as Berkeley Research, Rocket Lawyer, and Eden McCallum have stronger controls—without unwieldy bureaucracies, it must be said—that provide them with platforms for further expansion. BSO is a tragic in-between: as the company grew beyond national borders, its limited control system, which was originally underpinned by strong cultural ties, was unable to support the expansion.

Control has its price, however. Leadership and staff have to spend more time "doing business with themselves," with an ensuing loss of entrepreneurial opportunity and flexibility. The professional community then has a continuous balancing act between being too loosely organized and not realizing enough benefits for its members (who then leave the community), and too much control, which sets the community on the slippery slope toward a corporate bureaucracy.[5]

---

[5] Volberda (1998), Es-Sajjade et al. (2021).

References

Armour, J., & Sako, M. (2020). AI-enabled business models in legal services: From traditional law firms to next-generation law companies? *Journal of Professions and Organization, 7*(1), 27–46.

Broderick, M. (2011). *The art of managing professional services. Insights from the leaders of the world's top firms*. Prentice Hall.

Es-Sajjade, A., Pandza, K., & Volberda, H. (2021). Growing pains: Paradoxical tensions and vicious cycles in new venture growth, *Strategic Organization, 19*(1): 37–69.

Fiol, C. M., & Romenelli, E. (2012). Before identity: The emergence of new organizational forms. *Organizational Science, 23*(3), 507–611.

Volberda, H. W. (1998). *Building The Flexible Firm: How To Remain Competitive*. Oxford University Press.

Wintzen, E. (2006). *Eckart's notes*. Lemniscaat.

4

The Professional Service Community: The Way Forward

4.1 What the Professional Service Community Looks like and how it Works

4.1.1 From Firm to Community

In the preceding chapters, we have concluded that existing archetypes of professional services are less and less satisfactory. The gentlemen's club is too inflexible, the corporation bureaucratic, and flexfirms too undisciplined and too strongly oriented toward the short term. We need a business model that combines the small-size team spirit of the gentlemen's club with the wide and deep resource pool of the professional corporation and the entrepreneurial network of the flexfirm. And a model that enables us to provide top-level services in a very cost-effective way while creating a climate that supports innovation. That is possible, and we call it *the professional service community*.

In future we will provide our professional services through a community of independent firms. Each has between 5 and 100 people who know each other well. Long experience shows that people know each other reasonably well in a team of up to 100 people—as in the logic of military organization from Roman times onward. Our firms make work arrangements with other firms that have complementary talents and skills, and deliver complementary services. This community of firms shares a limited number of work rules and a culture. The result is an integrated package of offerings that is provided by our community of firms. Cooperation between these teams is based on work agreements, but even more on a clear shared vision about what our community and its members want to achieve. This vision can relate to the role that the community wants to play in a market or arena—"we want to be the best professionals in transportation," or "finance." Or to a more general goal: "we want to help developing countries." Or even a short-term members' objective, like "we want to maximize the success/profitability of our member firms." It is up to the community members to decide which vision is most motivating and sustainable.

The community has a common brand and a common reputation outside. The binding and driving force is a shared ambition to use strong synergies between one or more of the business model elements. Agreements in our community are enforced by a small but effective leadership which has its own resources. Violations of the few rules that the community has are countered by sanctions. The leadership is controlled

4 The Professional Service Community: The Way Forward   87

in turn by a supervisory team that represents the members. Apart from the rules necessary to maintain the community's brand and synergy, subsidiarity prevails: the community only takes responsibility for those matters that are necessary to achieve the common goals and the agreed strategy. Clarity is needed in the brand and positioning of both the community and its individual participants. After all, the member firms are free to serve their own clients and to develop their own services with their own business model.

The members will each have their own sub-brand. An example of community brand versus individual brands could be as follows:

GoldenEagle—Professionals for the Construction Industry (brand of the community) with the following members:

- GoldenEagle Strategy—member of GoldenEagle.
- Hawk and Partners—training, associated with GoldenEagle.
- GABA accountancy—member of GoldenEagle.
- P-Control—project management for construction industry—member of GoldenEagle.

Different backgrounds – one brand!

Once a prospect for a contract has been picked up by a member of the community, the leadership appoints an account leader. Colleagues join in to provide guidance in selling the contract, customer contacts, and project execution. When the contract has been signed, the community leadership takes the initiative in forming the most appropriate group of community members to do the job, a "pop-up" project team specially organized for this assignment.

The unique quality of the community is the clarity of its multidisciplinary network. From the first day onward, there is a clear differentiation between the community and its constituent firms. This is different from today's large corporate firms, in which a variety of activities are carried out within one organization with large staff departments in place to realize a common strategy and synergy between the units. The community also is very different from the non-committal free-for-all networks that we so often see in the global alliances of medium-sized firms. It is clear how the leaders of the community control it and intervene in case of deviations from the quality standards and other essential rules that allow the community to function.

The professional community combines the qualities of the business models that are now in vogue for professional services. A well-functioning community has the collegial trust that characterizes the classic gentleman's club. At the same time, the community integrates this with the scale that is characteristic of the large multinational corporation. Moreover, the community also has the flexibility that we see in some newer firms that work with flex workers, the flexfirms. The client gets to do business with a community with a recognized brand, well-directed account management, project management, and central accounts settlement. If run well, the community can if needed achieve the same functional and geographic scope as a professional corporation, but with much more flexibility, more creativity and entrepreneurship, and much lower costs.

The diagram below illustrates the concept of the professional community (see Fig. 4.1).

In a professional community, we see that each of the functions of the business model described in the preceding chapters is performed by its member firms, from recruiting brainpower to managing knowledge, organizing, and keeping the finances running. And each function is subject to a certain measure of adjustment to make it fit in with the community goals. However, one goal of the community is to minimize these changes through subsidiarity, which means maximum independence and

4 The Professional Service Community: The Way Forward

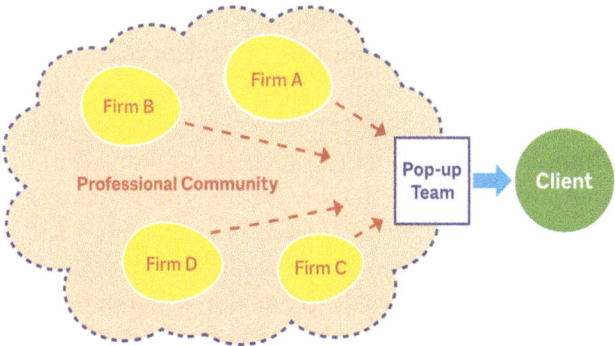

Fig. 4.1 The professional community

changes only where essential. The members can and will have their own individual *vision and strategy*, but if they want to be part of a community, these must be aligned with the vision and strategy of the group. Conflicts will be resolved for the benefit of the community. The same applies to policy with regard to clients and to the *brand and reputation* management of the community or the individual firm that forms part of it.

For two other functions—*brainpower* and *knowledge*—openness and sharing are essential, but these functions can be carried out with greater flexibility and freedom for the participating firm. With the other functions in the business model, such as *services*, *skills*, *organization*, and *economics*, the participants in the community are free to interpret them as they wish, provided they do not impede the interests and policies of the community.

4.2 The Community Has a Future, unlike the Old Archetypes

For most firms, the community is a more attractive prospect than the corporation, the gentlemen's club, or the flexfirm. The community has a strong and explicit vision of what it wants to achieve, central leadership, and a strong brand and reputation—all supported by its own budget and management structure. But at the same time, a professional community limits the requirements for a common vision, leadership, brand, and budget to those areas that are not part of its defined mission and scope. The individual members retain complete freedom to decide how to brand, lead, manage, and budget their other activities, as long as they remain within the overall bounds of their community. And they are free to be as innovative as they need to be. A community thus responds to the current trend toward minimal, "subsidiary" supervision and maximum self-management. After all, professionals who are aligned with a common vision and values are very well able to function with minimal control. The community is attractive to clients because of its flexibility and the ability to rapidly form an effective team with a broad skills base and low costs, while still being able to continue working with one contract partner.

4.3   Vision, Leadership, and the Pop-Up Team

4.3.1   What Should the Leadership of our Community Look like?

The community is a group of independent companies operating with limited but effective leadership that helps the members of the community reinforce the vision that brought them together, realizes the synergies that they are hoping for, and makes sure that the rules of the game that they agreed to are enforced. The leadership of our community has to play a directive role in areas such as reputation, quality, and standards.[1] To fulfill these functions, the leaders of our community need resources and power. Resources are in the form of staff and funding, and these can be provided, for example, through a levy on the members of a percentage of sales. Directive power can only be effective if sanctions are available, such as financial penalties or exclusion from the community. It must be possible to intervene if participants do not support the brand or do not meet the standards or quality of our community.[2,3]

---

[1] Weick (1982), Drucker (1996), Maister (1993).
[2] Delong et al. (2007).
[3] Bass (1990).

4.3.2 Coordination of Accounts and the Pop-up Project

The second key leadership function is the appointment and supervision of the project leadership. Every key account has an account coordinator who is appointed by the community leaders. The account coordinator is a linchpin in the community's revenue generation. The coordinator's job starts with marketing, network building, and sales to the client—on behalf of the entire community. When a project is sold, the account coordinator either takes overall charge of the project or proposes a colleague as project manager who—if the project is of a certain size—is again approved by the community leader. The account coordinator makes sure that the right partners are invited to join in the pop-up team in order to sell the job and to execute it.

Aha – the perspectives and energy of the leader!

This places high demands on professional salesmanship: externally in dealing with the client and internally when the pop-up team has to be assembled. Each unit leader may be expected to want to keep his own star staff members for himself, and it is the role of the project manager to help participating firms understand why they should assign their best people to the project.[4] We call it a pop-up team because we put the team together in an ad hoc way to sell and carry out a particular project. The next assignment for the next client can be expected to have a different team composition. Unit managers, who are usually managing partners of community member firms, should be rewarded for their contribution to pop-up teams.

4.4 Sources of Professional Value: Brainpower, Skills, and Knowledge

Professional success starts with having the right people. When those people are provided with the necessary skills and access to the knowledge they need to do their job, success is almost assured…

Brainpower… many are called, few are chosen

4.4.1 Finding and Retaining Brainpower in our Community

In every discussion with a managing director of a professional organization, the subject comes up of how to recruit and retain qualified employees. After all, any battle in the competitive marketplace can be won with

---

[4] Empson (2017).

good people. In the past, most graduates of law faculties preferred law firms, young economists were on their way to accountancy, and business administration graduates would end up in consultancy. Nowadays, these career choices are no longer self-evident.

Professional service communities make it possible to work in small units of a manageable size and with a high level of entrepreneurship, and thus cater to the preferences of NewGen. These can then provide manpower and creativity to the more established members of the community and the pop-up projects/teams. Conversely, the more established members can provide coaching and interesting career paths to the juniors who want to move beyond their small team. However, it will require a willingness within the community to share manpower and skills among the members. In this joint training, joint project work and coaching are important tools.

4.4.2 Skills and Capabilities

We have the best people and the best knowledge, but our company still has no services, no clients, and we have not yet achieved anything for our client. How do we convert our brainpower, information, and knowledge into something that the client needs and can be enthusiastic about? This requires skills from the people and the organization, and the capability to renew those skills. And a professional community can only function if it finds ways to effectively share and disseminate these skills between its members.

Skills can be seen as the ability of professionals to perform their specific role, to do their job, and to be successful. In other words: the combination of theoretical and practical knowledge, behavior, and values that are used to improve performance.[5] Everything that turns a smart novice into a capable senior.

Many professional firms manage their skills in an intuitive way.[6] These skills are often not made explicit, with the risk that they will not be passed

---

[5] Doz (1994), Van Wijk et al. (2005).
[6] Empson (2001), Maister (1993).

on properly to subsequent generations and will then be lacking at the crucial moment. It is not easy to renew skills. For example, the gentlemen's club is led by senior partners for whom it is usually difficult to form a picture of the future professional world with the corresponding skills.

In the case of a corporation, the complication is that we are dealing with a more complex organization, with several stakeholders and several staff functions, each with its own interests. For the future, it is necessary to adjust to a new way of working, with new skills, but again, this is not easy. On the other hand, there also is a problem with flexfirms. Participating professionals have no obligation toward the firm as a whole when they want to develop and disseminate new skills, making it difficult for management to launch these types of change processes. Due to its simple and clear structure in the chosen fields, a professional community has the combination of motivation and flexibility that makes it better able to quickly develop and spread new skills.[7]

---

[7] Prahalad and Hamel (1994), Van der Mandele et al. (2019).

4.4.3 How Do we Acquire New Skills?

The community offers a structure for acquiring skills and thus has an excellent dynamic capability. After all, if certain skills are lacking in the community, it can immediately establish a connection with a firm that does have those skills. Such a new partner will often have its own business model—think of cloud startups—and the community has the capability to integrate that model into its own, which is a much more difficult process for the more traditional archetypes.[8]

4.4.4 Knowledge in our Community

If we want to manage knowledge in our community effectively, we must start with the realization that there is a hierarchy in knowledge. At the bottom are figures, facts, and data. Once that data has been selected and sorted to such an extent that it is useful, it has become information. The transition from data to information requires structure.[9] If we then edit and interpret that information, it becomes know-how. This process requires analysis and synthesis. And if we formulate an opinion based on know-how, we can speak of insight and even wisdom. There also are different sources of knowledge. There is knowledge that comes from the public domain, such as law articles, regulations, market statistics, and websites. There is client information and knowledge, and internal firm information and knowledge, which often is confidential. This distinction largely determines whether we want to develop that knowledge ourselves or buy it from outside.[10]

Increasingly, knowledge is instantly accessible for everyone—and cheap! But extraction, selection, and interpretation are usually needed to turn raw data into useable information and knowledge. Furthermore, knowledge about clients and the firm itself is usually confidential.

---

[8] Teece (2003).
[9] Ackoff (1989).
[10] Chen et al. (2012).

Examples could be a client's cost data, a negotiating position, or profit prospects. Confidential knowledge and insight usually have market value because they enable us to help the client—or the competition—for which we could demand a financial reward.[11] The two dimensions of knowledge—from data to insight on the one hand and from public to your own firm on the other—can be projected in the diagram below (see Fig. 4.2). This classification also gives a clue as to where we can best find that knowledge. Valuable public data can usually be purchased at a low cost in the open market. Examples are national statistics and case law. The valuable insight into a client situation is knowledge that we can best gather and save ourselves.

Between these two categories of knowledge lies the "zone" where we can reduce costs by working in a community.[12]

---

[11] Morris (2001).
[12] Sarvary (1999).

Sourcing knowledge

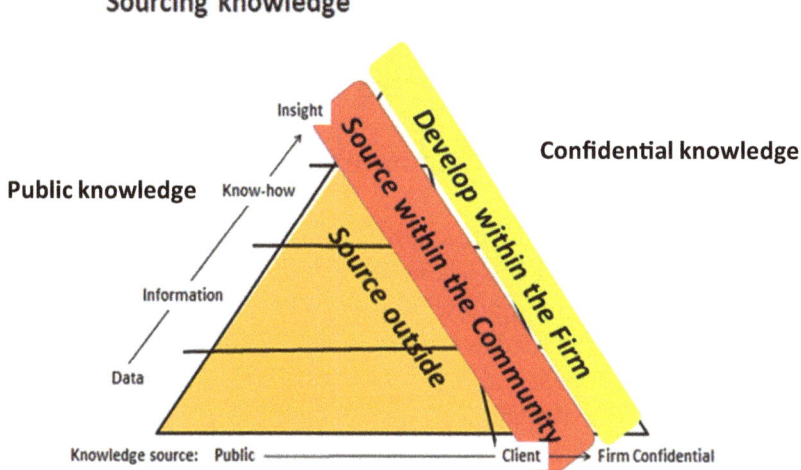

Fig. 4.2 Sourcing knowledge

It is here that the community can prove its worth. After all, investment in knowledge can be shared by the community. Specialization can occur where one participant manages a database for the entire group and a vast information base can support both larger members and innovative start-ups within the community. This is possible because the community creates a basis of trust in which partnerships can share confidential knowledge without risk.[13] To be able to realize the enormous positive knowledge management potential of our community, three conditions must be met.

First, there must be total *connectivity* between the knowledge and skills of the different community members. This implies excellent information and communications interconnect.

We also need a healthy *trust* base in the community. Otherwise, the community partners will not want to share knowledge with each other.

And finally, there must be strict *rules* and a certain degree of central management to ensure security and financing of knowledge development.[14]

---

[13] Morris and Empson (1998).
[14] Davenport (2005).

4.5 Creating Professional Value through Organization, Good Economics, and the Right Culture

4.5.1 Organizing our Community

Organization comprises the structure and processes with which the community operates. We are not talking about the management of the partner firms within the community. They control themselves.

But the community needs a few processes to guide its members. These relate to the governance and management of the vision, policy, reputation, and quality of the community as a whole. But leadership cannot work in a vacuum. It must be nourished by the opinions that live in the community. And it must be accountable to the participants. This requires supervision. In the case of the community, it is desirable for this supervision to function compactly and efficiently, so that the community is not burdened with a heavy structure.

4.5.2 How Should we Govern our Community?

Good governance starts with finding the right governors, which is a result of a good selection process. Because the governance of a community will only impose its will in a limited number of areas—we mentioned brand, quality, and account management—the board will have to rely to some extent on charisma and diplomacy to represent the interests of the community among its members. Self-interest will also motivate community participants to accept a central government. This means it is best if directors come from their own community because they have their network and internal reputation ready. The administrators must be visionary, but at the same time they must be able to handle the peculiarities of each of the participants. That is certainly a challenging combination of qualities.

Management of the community must be light. The professionals in the different firms usually already find the overhead of their own management and staff burdensome. Therefore, it may be useful to ask leaders of participating firms to rotate in leading the community for a number of years. The managing partner or former managing partners of participating firms are particularly eligible for this. Advantages of this approach are that contact with the participants is ensured and it is very probable that the appointee will be considered credible by his or her colleagues. And this structure does not have to be expensive. A disadvantage is that a rotating daily management often has less clout than a more permanent position. And there is less time to develop and execute a new strategy.

As stated, community governance must have strength in a small number of important areas. We mentioned brand and account management, and service quality. That power requires leverage: a carrot for those who do well and a stick behind the door for those who break the rules. The best way to organize this is to pass all revenues through the community office. In this way, the leadership can intervene in the event of abuses relating to the income of the participating firms. A less good alternative is to have each participant pay a fixed fee to the head office.

The third alternative is to give the community leadership a voice in the partner meetings of each participating firm.

4.6 Creating the "Superculture" in the Community

Culture is the glue that keeps the community going in the many day-to-day processes that we do not want to micro-manage. But the complexity of the topic becomes clear when we realize how many different types of culture can coexist in our community. Some participants will function in a tight hierarchy, while others will be driven from the shop floor as an "adhocracy." Some participants will move flexibly in line with the latest market fads, while others will follow their own beliefs as they invest in the future needs of the market. And if our organization extends across several countries, the culture discussion is complicated further.[15] In a community, the cultures will differ, but they must be compatible.[16] A professional firm that is dominated by a few seniors will have to cooperate with a firm in which the juniors have a lot of leeway. But there are limits to cultural diversity. A firm that puts business above all else and cares less about ethics will have a hard time working together with a firm that places high demands on its social behavior and cares about the environment.[17]

The leadership of the community has the challenging task of giving all those cultural patterns their individual freedom while encouraging them to work together in a "superculture." Not only should the cultures of the participants in a community not rub against each other too much, but the commonality of values and behavioral habits will also have to lead to a *common* culture to be imposed on the individual cultures of the participating companies: a "superculture." This culture of the community has to be a culture that can (and must) be encouraged by the leadership of the members.

A complication here is that the leadership of the community must continue to respect the individuality of the participants.[18]

4.6.1 How Do we Build our "Superculture"?

The challenge facing the leadership of a community in building a common culture lies in the elusiveness of culture. Instructions to change culture issued from above only lead to limited behavioral changes among employees. And since the leadership of a community is more remote, these changes are even harder to achieve. Furthermore, these changes

---

[15] Trompenaars and Hampton Turner (1993).
[16] Kotter and Heskett (1992).
[17] Deal and Kennedy (1982).
[18] Cameron and Quinn (1999).

4 The Professional Service Community: The Way Forward

have to be compatible with the way members work. After all, the intention is not to destroy the character of the member firm in the process.

For starters: a sine qua non for a good community culture is a clear *vision* for the mission, values, and rules of conduct. This should be clearly communicated to the professionals who manage the individual members of the community, but also to other stakeholders such as clients and contractors. These cultural rules will only work if the leadership sets the example. For example, if ethics is an important part of the community's vision and management allows its staff to give clients exorbitant gifts, the credibility of the community will quickly disappear.

The next important topic is joint *training*. Learning and working together in a training program will build bonds between community professionals that will prove their value in running projects and realizing synergies. This training program should not limit itself to general professional skills such as team and project management, verbal and written communications, and marketing and sales. The participating firms may already take sufficient care of these competencies and subsequent training. Training of participants could focus more on the peculiarities of working in multidisciplinary teams and on basic knowledge of the services of the firms participating in the community. Pop-up teams may engage in team-building exercises. In addition, seniors from participating firms will join in for "fireside chats" about vision, mission, ethics, and other culture-related topics.

Mixing the ingredients that make our superculture

Mixed task forces comprising members from the different community units are a perfect way to ensure that the proposals they develop are acceptable and accepted across the community. And the members of these task forces will get to know and appreciate each other, which will create and facilitate opportunities to work together on projects. Finally, rituals and traditions are valuable for underpinning the community culture. Examples are the annual summer party or winter conference for the partners of the community, the symbolic gift on the occasion of a promotion to partner, or the award for the most customer-oriented action of the employees. There is a delicate balance to be achieved between actively building the community "superculture" and respecting the identity of its members. Subsidiarity above all!

4.7 How to Make Money with our Community

As mentioned above, our community has a common vision, but at the same time it owes its success to its flexibility. The question is how flexible the economic model must and can be and how we can organize it. At the same time, the community needs money to pay for central coordination of common tasks such as marketing, IT, and training. This requires money and staff. If the participants want to work closely together and respond effectively to market dynamics, the flow of money should go through the community leadership, which can take the form of a common legal entity of which the participants are shareholders. The community leadership will then also be given powers to impose discipline in the application of the agreed vision, values, and rules of conduct. Moreover, in this way the community leadership has easy access to the resources necessary for joint activities, and also for building up a capital balance that is in any case needed for debt financing. Because in this case the client only gets one invoice, the brand is supported and the payments are simplified. This is easiest when all members have the same earnings method, e.g., by using hourly fees. Contract and tariff differences between the participants must be settled afterward.[19]

There is a more decentralized alternative where the "pop-up" firm manages the assignment, makes the arrangements, and sends the invoices.

---

[19] Teece (2003).

4 The Professional Service Community: The Way Forward

This produces a much more dynamic picture. Different contract forms can then be used for pricing and risk-sharing. The project manager must then collect the common costs, administer the agreements and payments with all participating firms, and bear the debtor risk of the client.

The most decentralized form leaves it to every participant in a project to contract with the client independently. This variant offers maximum flexibility and the opportunity to contractually tailor every part of the project. In this case, a project organization is conceivable whereby some parts of the work can be charged per hour and others at a fixed or variable price. The most decentralized form also makes it easy to deviate from the standard remuneration scheme for certain parts of a project, for example, for a capital participation. This model does not really support the image and functioning of one team, which is a strong element of the way a professional community works.

The diagram below shows how different priorities when setting up the community lead to different forms of economic management and enable different contract forms (see Fig. 4.3).

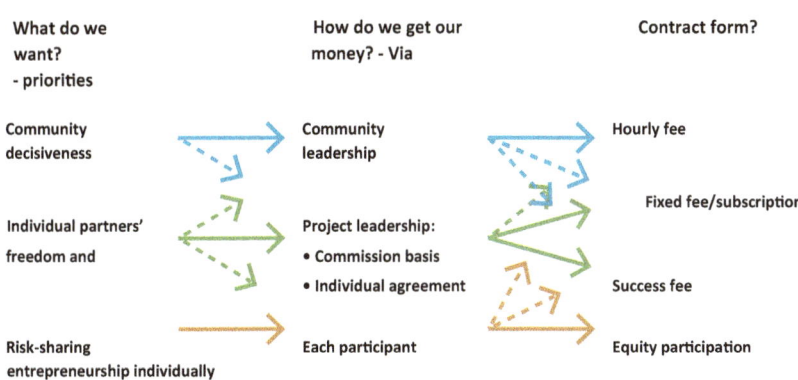

Fig. 4.3 Choosing the right contract form

4.7.1 Work Steps to Arrive at the Appropriate Economic Model

In the previous section, we saw that there is a whole range of possible earnings models for the community. How can we as a community determine what our specific economic arrangement should look like? To begin with, we must again stress the importance of alignment between the community members regarding the vision, priorities, and rules of the community. The rules provide answers to questions such as how projects are sold and who negotiates the contracts, how projects will be managed and who pays if things go wrong, and how payment will be made. If a start has been made with the wrong economic rules, it is very difficult to reverse things and reform those rules. If those principles are clear, it is best to find out first what kind of contract forms—fee, fixed price, risk-bearing, or capital participation—the community and each member wants to use. It can then be determined whether the cash flow can best be managed centrally or decentrally. If a central institution is chosen, then the capital needs of this central organization, management and supervision, access, and exit rules will have to be considered. Once all that is clear, the design of the model can be started and operational matters such as the legal form and staffing can be completed.

4.8 Reputation as the Sustainable Foundation of our Community

4.8.1 Reputation Is the Name of the Game

Without a sound reputation, your introductory letter will disappear into "file #7" without being read by the corporate manager to whom you wrote it. Without a reputation, you may be able to convince your counterpart at the client of the qualities of your proposal, but not the people around him or her. Without a reputation, you will probably be thrown out at the first mistake that your team makes. And without a reputation, your bright applicant will have to explain to family and friends why he opted for a job at your firm instead of famous "brand x."[20] Reputation reflects the opinions in the market about our firm. These opinions are held not only by potential clients, but also and especially by potential employees.

Reputation concerns the services we offer, our value proposition, the way we work, the type of clients and employees we have, and the image that the outside world has of our mission.

Brand –your shining light

---

[20] Langham (2018).

Reputation starts with the brand and the brand should open the door. The important functions of a brand include the name, design, symbols, or other characteristics that distinguish the firm from the competition in the eyes of potential customers, potential employees, and the general public. The brand begins with a description of the service and its characteristics, followed closely by the benefits of the service for the client, the prospective employee, and the public. The brand also expresses the values, capabilities, and personality of a service. The values and personality of a brand can indicate many emotions, such as integrity, competence, quality, and robustness. But also excitement, class, or style. Clients look for the personality they aspire to in a brand.

A client who wants to show that he is looking "higher up" will go for a big-city firm, whereas a client who wants to present himself internationally is willing to pay for a firm with an international brand. Sometimes the brand and reputation disappear, and consequently their market value. Who remembers once "blue chip" names such as Dewey Leboeuf in law, Braxton in consulting, or Arthur Andersen in accounting?

4.8.2 Reputation: A Special Challenge for our Community

Reputation and brand requires a lot of attention from a professional community.[21] On the one hand, a community can only compete with corporates and gentlemen's clubs if it has a strong and reasonably homogeneous (and not confusing) brand. On the other hand, community participants, each with its own business model and mission, must serve their own clients and recruit their own people. They therefore have their own reputation, which can be better supported by their own sub-brand. In this way, a regional firm in a community can emphasize local contacts and insights into regional business, while at the same time making strong and supportive noises about the values and mission of the community of firms in which it participates. In industry the use of sub-brands has

---

[21] Fombrun and Shankey (1990).

4 The Professional Service Community: The Way Forward

proven very effective. The Volkswagen group of operating companies, for example, benefits from the confidence that buyers have in German engineering even if they buy a sporty Spanish SEAT, a prestigious Audi, or a solid and relatively inexpensive Skoda. The same applies to customers of cosmetics and food giant Unilever who buy Dove, Knorr, Omo, and Lipton, trusting the quality and product performance of a Unilever product. In professional services, we see that consultancy firm Booz & Company has changed its name to &Strategy and continues under the reputation of PWC. To be successful, a community will have to think hard about the brand and its family of sub-brands that fit together and reinforce each other, while emphasizing the reputation of the community its participants.

Build a brand from different backgrounds…

4.9 Delivering Value with our Community

4.9.1 Which Services we Want to Deliver with our Community

The big question for our professional community and its management is thus: in which services should we invest? And are there services that we should terminate? The community and its participants must have a clear view of their work portfolio if they are to sustain their business in the long run. And their desired work portfolio decides their membership. To start with, it is better to invest in services that have a positive market perspective. That means, among other things:

- Growth. Decline almost always leads to more competition and lower rates.
- Not too much competition. That can also mean: be careful with tenders that can lead to a downward spiral in contract prices.
- Good margins. These are often associated with the complexity of the work. Too little complexity—such as a standard legal document or audit—means price competition and the risk of automation. Too much complexity—such as a large multinational engagement or a highly specialized job—means that a large corporate or a small expert firm will get the order.

It is important for our community that the service package that we offer matches the competencies of our participants. Competencies are a function of the kind of people that the community participants employ (i.e., our brainpower), the skills that the participating companies have taught them, and the knowledge that those people possess. These competencies are closely related to the business model of the community participants. Finally, it is also important for the attractiveness of a service for our community whether it can lead to further work. If we do a one-off job, such as providing expertise in a legal conflict, then there is perhaps only a small chance that the client will return for more projects in other areas. If, on the other hand, we conduct a strategic audit on an annual basis, this opens the doors to opportunities to address further problems that are identified. This, incidentally, may lead to regulatory problems for the auditors.

The most difficult position is when a good market prospect emerges, but there is initially only a modest fit with the competencies and resources of our community. It is here that the unique character of the professional community demonstrates its value.

After all, every professional firm has the possibility to build a new service by starting an innovation process. However, we must realize that an innovation process requires considerable resources, attention, and time, and entails risks—risks that are often underestimated. Furthermore, every firm can make an acquisition, with all the associated risks: market risk and synergy risk, to name just two. The community is flexible and has a unique ability to enable participants to find their most productive positions within the group, in a way that suits them best, and to find new members that add needed competencies. This means that resources, time, and risks are kept to a minimum.[22]

4.10 A Promising List of Clients

We can only be successful with our community if we have a list of promising and loyal clients with whom we can do good business on a sustainable basis. These clients rarely knock on our door. We therefore risk chasing after clients who are ultimately not interested in our competences and way of working. The parties that do knock on the door do not always generate interesting work with which we can earn our living. We will therefore have to make the necessary effort to find and win the right clients.

Let us start with *attractiveness*. Good sales volume and a regular sales flow from a client means reliable revenues that help community members invest in top-quality staff and new services. This may point to larger customers who are frequent users of external professional support, but also

---

[22] Treacy and Wiersema (1995).

have a tendency to organize shoot-outs or tenders between competitors which are expensive and risky.

But this sales flow can come from a large population of clients, each of which occasionally places small orders, as exemplified by the small-town lawyer who has a long list of retail customers.

The second dimension is *fit*. A good relationship potential means that we are dealing with a client with whom we can build a relationship of trust, with clear and effective communications. That does not mean that the client accepts all our work without question, but it does mean that clarity and predictability enable us to work together quickly and efficiently. The ideal client therefore regularly has assignments for us, which we can handle quickly and effectively with a minimum of friction. When we combine high attractiveness and good fit, we can represent that client as an elephant in the figure below. If the client offers us too little work, we will see him more as a rabbit. If that client comes to us, we will want to help, but we will not spend too much on marketing and relationship management.

Much lower in our ranking are clients with a critical approach, with whom we have much less fit and have to negotiate continuously during the sale and during the work. If they are economically attractive, we call them tigers. There often is little pleasure in working for them, although sometimes we cannot avoid them for other reasons. If they generate little turnover, we call them rats and we prefer to avoid them.

4 The Professional Service Community: The Way Forward

At the very bottom of the table are the tenders, which are rarely attractive, if only because the probability of actually winning the proposal is low and average expenses per tendered proposal high (see Fig. 4.4). And if many firms participate in the tender market, they risk ending in a downward revenue spiral. Illustrative in that context was the announcement by EY in 2017 that it had become the market leader in Europe by focusing on larger commercial companies and by reducing its involvement in the municipal market, where tenders are mainly used. Many professionals consider tenders "the pits," with the exception of those firms that have successfully mastered the intricacies of tendering and sometimes make money from it.

The final selection of clients is a pragmatic one and relates to *accessibility*. In most professional work, it is desirable for the client to be within easy communicating distance of our professionals (although advances in IT make physical distance less of a problem). However, this accessibility is not only physical: approaching a new client or maintaining the relationship is much easier if the leadership and other key figures already

Fig. 4.4 Interesting clients

belong to our professional and social networks. We work on our network with our potential clients, and this is therefore part of our community's marketing program. We prefer to build on that network long before we are in a sales situation and our potential client has adopted a critical purchasing attitude. There are many different non-selling ways to build a client network. This includes seminars, user forums, industry meetings, industry research, market research, and client feedback. In this way, we move from a world of potential clients to a specific target group—a list of organizations on which we want to focus our marketing and sales efforts.

The marketing/sales phase will probably involve different members to build the necessary network at the client and develop the proposal. Collegiality in the community and coordination by the central unit will be necessary to ensure that synergy is realized and common resources are mobilized. This starts with the appointment of an account coordinator and pop-up team by the community leadership. When contracting with the client, one of the community's participants, or the community leadership, will have to take the lead in making agreements for all. Once the work has been done and delivered, it is not only necessary to pay, but also to manage the client's network on behalf of the community, and to see where the next assignment lies and who will take the lead in it. These are processes in which the management and culture of the community are put to the test.

> **Do I Want to Join a Firm?**
> Times are confusing for young professionals who want to become lawyers, consultants, or accountants. They have so many options: a large international firm, a specialized boutique, a local firm. Or a loosely connected network, or even as an independent? These all are serious possibilities, each with its pros and cons of course. We delve into the matter and even provide advice!
> **On your own it is difficult to grow as professional**
> Professionals organize themselves in many different structures and forms, each of which can be successful. Recent years have only seen an increase in the variety of ways in which people find their way from rags to riches. The independent practitioner has, for example, become quite popular in recent times, enabled by Internet marketing, online databases, and easy
>
> *(continued)*

(continued)
communications. In this environment, the added value of a firm is under question. This explains why the 2008–2012 crisis, with its shake-out of large firms, also demonstrated how easily the better professionals can establish their own practice. Although the independent practitioner has been around since professions originated, it appears that the one-person practice and network models are gaining in popularity. Reason enough to consider the firm and see whether it makes any sense for a younger professional to sign up.

The arguments:
- Apprenticeship leads to mastery.
  If you believe that university is not enough to become really good, that combining theory and practice can only be learned by doing and that personal growth is essential for mastering professional wisdom, then a learning environment is needed. The medieval guilds provide an interesting reference point.
- Learning the hard way.
  Many professionals thrive on peer interaction in which they can test out their thoughts without being penalized. Real learning often happens the hard way—within the team. Without teamwork, a lone professional achieves mixed results in a wobbly career.
- A broader horizon.
  Independent professionals often develop a short-term view of clients and prospects. After all, their income for the next few months depends on the next assignment. Their focus on the job at hand is both their strength and weakness. But in many cases, they do not have the time to develop a long-term strategy with their clients and market.
- Identity and belonging.
  Professionals are human and enjoy being part of an identified group which gives them a name to stand for and a home group of peers. Trust also enables synergy between the members of the team.
- Reputation.
  A firm has the resources to develop a reputation that stretches beyond individuals and beyond the immediate term. This also enables the senior to recruit colleagues and thus leverage his name with obvious financial benefits. This explains why famous lawyers, business consultants, and accountants end up establishing teams.
- The edge in quality.
  Seniors and a team of trusted professional colleagues will also act as a sounding board and guide when quality standards are breached.

(continued)

> **(continued)**
>
> **New models, old ruths**
> In conclusion, think twice before venturing out on your own after graduation or your first years in a firm. I have seen the excitement of many colleagues during their first months of going solo. But after the first few happy years, I have also seen what I call their professional loneliness: the challenge of keeping up with clients, markets, and new methodologies as they run to make ends meet in the immediate term. They neglect marketing and sales, and their engagement pipelines become shorter and shorter. Not to mention their specialty becoming outdated.
>
> My advice: make the right choice before this happens. Choose a setting that suits you. And why not make this a firm—a great setting for your professional career!

References

Ackoff, R. L. (1989). From data to wisdom. In *Journal of systems analysis*. Cited in: *Ackoffs best* (pp. 170–172). Wiley.

Bass, B. M. (1990). From transactional to transformational leadership: Learning to share the vision. *Organizational Dynamics, 18*(3), 19–31.

Cameron, K. S., & Quinn, R. E. (1999). *Diagnosing and changing organizational culture*. Prentice Hall.

Chen, H. M., Chian, H. I., & Stacey, V. C. (2012). Business intelligence – From big data to big impact. *MIS Quarterly, 36*(4), 1165–1188.

Davenport, T. H. (2005). *Thinking for a living: How to get better performance and results from knowledge workers*. Harvard Business School Press.

Deal, T. E., & Kennedy, A. A. (1982). *Corporate cultures: The rites and rituals of corporate life*. Addison-Wesley.

DeLong, T. J., Gabarro, J. J., & Lees, R. J. (2007). *When professionals have to Lead*. Harvard Business School Press.

Doz, Y. (1994). *Managing Core competencies for corporate renewal: Towards a managerial theory of Core competencies*. Insead Working Papers, 94/23/SM.

Drucker, P. F. (1996). Your leadership is unique. *Christianity Today International/Leadership Journal, 17*(4), 54–55.

Empson, L. (2001). Knowledge management in professional service firms. *Human Relations, 11*(2), 39–46.

Empson, L. (2017). *Leading professionals: Power, politics and prima donnas.* Oxford University Press.

Fombrun, C., & Shankey, M. (1990). What's in the name? Reputation building and corporate strategy. *Academy of Management Journal, 33*(2), 233–258.

Langham, T. (2018). *Reputation management: The future of corporate communications and public relations.* Emerald Publishing.

Kotter, J. P., & Heskett, J. L. (1992). *Corporate culture and performance.* The Free Press.

Maister, D. H. (1993). *Managing the professional service firm.* The Free Press.

Morris, T., & Empson, L. (1998). Organization and expertise: An exploration of knowledge bases and the management of accounting and consulting firms. *Accounting, Organizations & Society, 23*, 609–624.

Morris, T. (2001). Asserting property rights: Knowledge codification in the professional service firm. *Human Relations, 54*, 819–838.

Prahalad, C. K., & Hamel, G. (1994). *Competing for the future.* Harvard Business School Press.

Sarvary, M. (1999). Knowledge management and competition in the consulting industry. *California Management Review, 41*(2), 95–107.

Teece, D. J. (2003). Expert talent and the design of professional service firms. *Industrial and Corporate Change, 12*(4), 895–916.

Treacy, M., & Wiersema, F. (1995). *The discipline of market leaders: Choose your customers, narrow your focus, dominate your market.* Perseus Books.

Trompenaars, F., & Hampton Turner, C. (1993). *Riding the waves of culture.* Economist Books.

Van der Mandele, L. M., Volberda, H. W., & Wagenaar, R. (2019). *De nieuwe professional service firm: Hoe advocaten, accountants, & adviseurs zichzelf opnieuw uitvinden.* Scriptum Publishers.

Van Wijk, R. van, Van den Bosch, F. A. J., Volberda, H. W. & Heinhuis, S. M. (2005). Knowledge Reciprocity as a Managerial Competence: The Determinants of Reciprocity of Knowledge Flows in Internal Network Forms of Organizing. In R. Sanchez and A. Heene (Eds.), *Research in Competence-Based Management*, (pp. 117–140). Elsevier.

Weick, K. H. (1982). Management of organizational change among loosely coupled elements. In P. S. Goodman et al. (Eds.), *Change in organizations, new perspectives in theory, research and practice* (pp. 375–409). Jossey Bass.

Six pillars of success

5

Foundations of the Successful Professional Community

5.1 Our Professional Community Needs Strong Foundations

In the preceding chapters, we introduced the community as a new way to overcome the disruptions that are threatening our professions. We also described the elements that together form the business model of our community. But we have not yet discussed the foundations that turn this model into a successful operation. Some of these are policies and even technical specifications—connection, compatibility, and commonality. Others are "soft" and cultural—trust, tolerance, and transparency. And some are economic—growth and innovation. They all add to the leverage of a successful community in the form of synergy. In the following pages, we will discuss the main foundations of success in a professional service community:

1. The three "C"s: connection, compatibility, and commonality.
2. A supportive group of community professionals.

3. Trust, tolerance, and transparency—the three "T"s.
4. Growth as a perennial driver of organizational success.
5. Synergy to build on the foundation and achieve success.
6. Innovation and renewal.

5.2 What Does Success Mean in a Community?

For a "normal" gentlemen's club or a professional corporation, the question of success may simply be that we let all our professionals benefit from our efforts in an equitable way. For a community, the question of success is more complicated, because we are dealing with a diverse group of independent companies. For some this means immediate profits, while for others it offers the prospect of a long-term reputation. Or it can simply be an enjoyable way to earn a living.

Every participant in the community has his or her own definition of success and sets his or her own priorities. It is important to initiate a discussion about this at the start of the community: on the one hand to define properly what success is for the group and each partner, and on the other hand to understand clearly where the differences between the participants lie. If we know and agree on what success is, we can decide on our milestones and yardsticks for progress.

5.3 Connectivity, Compatibility, and Commonality

5.3.1 Connectivity

The rapid rise of modern information and communications technology (ICT) in recent years has transformed our work situation. Gone are the days when information was gathered in libraries and interviews,

5 Foundations of the Successful Professional Community

analyses were done on paper at desks, and communications were maintained by telephone, fax, and courier. Screens make it possible to create a virtual office by linking spaces in different cities and countries. The potential of our professional service community is largely a consequence of the progress made in ICT. We can now work together remotely—continuously and intensively. We can now effectively mobilize large common databases. We can easily manage revenues and calculate equitable cost settlements between partners. IT has brought enormous changes and it continues to develop. Project platforms make it possible for different parties to develop and share information and knowledge in real time.

Connectivity starts with high-quality exchanges of information. That means either using the same software packages or at least making sure software can be seamlessly connected or is totally compatible. It also implies a certain level of standardization of technology and information. If partners working together use different meanings of the word "revenue" or billability/coverage, and different cutoff points for project start, end, and accounting periods, it complicates their cooperation to a level where they can no longer effectively align their thoughts and actions. A similar issue arises in the area of knowledge and information sharing. Partners should have as much access as possible to each other's projects, industries, and client data. None of this is easy, but to succeed, a professional community should not only take steps from the outset to achieve connectivity, but also to agree on a vision of where the members want to go.

Getting the connectivity right relates to the value sources of the community and its partners. It is a matter of aligning the people (the brainpower), making the skills work together, and tying together the knowledge bases.

5.3.2 Compatibility

Working together in a professional community is ultimately only successful if the vision, values, and business models of the community partners are compatible. For example, a collaboration between an idealistic, cooperatively organized firm and a firm where the partners' bonuses come first will sooner or later lead to irreconcilable conflicts. The compatibility requirement does not mean that the partners in the community must all have the same vision and values, only that the individual visions must support instead of contradict each other. Partners must also be able and willing to accept their differences, and we will talk about tolerance later.

Compatibility relates to the value-creation functions of the community and its partners, their organizations, their earnings models, and, in

5 Foundations of the Successful Professional Community

particular, their cultures have to be compatible. But more intangible functions, such as branding and the vision of the individual partners, have to be in harmony.

The same applies to the control systems. The leadership and partners of the community should understand how the different units are doing if they are to work together effectively in serving clients and in developing their community. That implies a single set of reporting standards for items such as bookings, revenues, operating margins, investments, and profits. There are many examples of professional firms that failed through a lack of good company-wide controls, for example, the global marketing firm WPP. Commonality of reporting definitions and guidelines will be the minimum.

Survival of the fitting

5.3.3 Commonality

Commonality starts with a strong shared vision about what the community wants to achieve and how it sees the scope of its activities. Scope is important for a community because of the ease with which it can expand its membership—that is, until it finds itself to be a loose agglomeration of unrelated activities.

The visions of the individual members can differ, as long as their shared vision of the community is unambiguous and supported by everyone. Furthermore, a successful community also shares a limited number of important functions. For example, the community can only operate effectively if it uses a common contracting policy for the outside world and between partners. Quality and quality assurance must be at a comparable level between the community partners.

Commonality relates to value delivery, i.e., the way in which clients are selected and the services are produced.

Diverse backgrounds – compatible results ...

5.3.4 Conclusion

Philippe Mauchard, one of the founders of McKinsey Solutions, states: "A sustainable community needs a brand, both for the client and for the recruitment market. Furthermore, the participants in the community have to trust each other in accepting a central economic control (e.g. because the turnover is administered by a lead firm) and management (e.g. equity investments). The community must be flexible (with always changing pop-up teams, for example). Finally, it must also have sound quality control and knowledge management."

The managing partner of a Big Four UK accounting firm adds: "Communities can be successful if they keep staff functions and overheads low, maintain strong cooperation and control their quality. Rules and reports do not help to get this right. What is needed are indirect means such as culture, training, coaching and exemplary behavior."

A strong brand and vision will make successful teamwork possible. The community's common resources can be invested in the community brand, marketing, and infrastructure. Investment in communications technology and personal connections is essential for much-needed team work and collegiality. That is the key to success in large, complex, or urgent projects.

5.4 The Successful Community Professional

As we all know, any business model can only flourish if the people working with and within this model have an attitude and behavior that supports it. Since the professional community differs considerably from the other archetypes of professional firms, it is worthwhile exploring what this community professional should look like.[1] It is quite a challenge to describe his or her features and competences. Can we identify a species called community professional? And if so, in which sense will that person be any different from any other successful professional?

People tend to work with what they have learnt in life, especially with what has made them successful. A successful consultant will rely on his

---

[1] Faulconbridge and Muzio (2008), Lorsch and Tierney (2002).

or her past experiences and so will a successful lawyer. When they do start working in their newly founded community, professionals will use their own history in approaching and adapting to this new model of working. A lot of them will see little or no reason to do anything differently. They earn their comfortable living and are successful and happy with their traditional work. Clients are satisfied and their old firms appreciate their performance. These are not the people who will drive the success of the community. Instead, the focus should be on the frontrunners who engage in building up the community and the client spearheads who identify the new assignments that need a team of community partners. Those account coordinators, often partners of firms or bright young men and women, will be crucial for the success of the model.

Venture your way through the jungle

5.4.1 What Characteristics Should we Expect Them to Have?[2]

5.4.1.1 Curious, Creative, Entrepreneurial

As both the way of working on assignments and the community model as such are new, professionals with the above characteristics are needed to

---

[2] Blomgren and Waks (2015).

give the community approach a chance. The challenge for the successful community professional is that most engagements will follow a new model and that this model is an innovation of a higher order. It needs people who can think and act at different levels of abstraction, who are interested in both the new model of the firm and new services for the client, and who are also capable of communicating and convincing others to follow their way of thinking.[3]

5.4.1.2 Positive, Optimistic, Can-Do Mentality, Persistent

Many hurdles must be overcome before the model will flourish: hurdles in the creation of the model, in identifying and scoping community assignments, in convincing the market and clients of the merits of this different approach, in working with groups of very different professionals/disciplines, and more. This calls for people who are determined to make the model a success, who are willing to commit their own boundless positive energy and who are resilient to setbacks and disappointments. Communities need these people to have a chance to flourish!

5.4.1.3 Communicative Leaders of People and Ideas

The community and its projects will need leaders who combine an inspiring vision with the communications skills needed to get people—both community colleagues and client staff – on board. As hierarchy is less strong in a community, the team's performance will depend more on the ability to explain the task at hand and to motivate the teammates to go after the result. We do not expect many professionals to be able to rise to this level and be the successful pioneers of the community. But as always, true innovation depends on a few. And it needs only a few to lead.

---

[3] Ibarra and Obodaru (2016), Senge et al. (1994).

5.5 Trust, Tolerance, and Transparency: Cornerstones of Culture

When professionals consider all the structural arrangements that must be made to set up a successful professional community, they often overlook cultural "soft" factors, even though these principles—trust, tolerance, and transparency—are of the utmost importance. These three are not so much related to systems, rules, or procedures but rather embody the behavior of the participants involved. We will address all three and try to describe why they are important in a community, what they look like when practiced, and what difficulties professionals have in acting in accordance with these principles.

5.5.1 Trust

Professionals need to be trusted when doing their complicated and highly skilled jobs for clients. After all, trust is often the main reason why a client selects a certain professional for an assignment! Without the trust of clients, it would be impossible to do an effective job. On the other hand, the client often has no option but to trust the professional, if only because of the client's limited understanding of the project topic—which is the reason for recruiting an expert in the first place.

5 Foundations of the Successful Professional Community

Strangely enough, the fact that professionals enjoy the trust of their clients does not necessarily mean that it is easy for them to trust their own colleagues. Many professionals have a very critical, sometimes even skeptical, mindset and question situations they are not familiar with or, in particular, their colleagues' insights. Even within a firm with a differentiated specialist portfolio, collaboration between experts is not easy. One of the reasons is doubtless that they usually have to rely on their own competences and experience when they face client questions. The better—and certainly easier—attitude is to speak with confidence from your own knowledge and not to risk trusting the unknown qualities of your colleagues.[4]

We can talk about collegial trust when team members deliver something to their colleagues without expecting to immediately receive a delivery in return. This is especially important in those cases where the delivery cannot be measured properly, if it is not clear who exactly delivers or how something is delivered, or if there are exogenous factors that make the delivery less visible. If cooperation is less clear-cut, action must be taken without the prospect of immediate compensation and without the need to monitor and control the colleague's work—in short, on a collegial basis. That emotional trust involves a much deeper relationship than rational trust. While a breach of rational trust is seen as a breach of contract and non-compliance with agreements, a breach of emotional collegiality is felt as a betrayal.[5]

---

[4] Gluckler and Armbruster (2003).
[5] Heckscher and Adler (2006).

A major reason for working with a community is that it enables different disciplines to work closely together to deliver a better job. And as the community is not organized through one firm, but through several independent firms, each of them with different competences, we can expect professionals to keep a critical eye on each other. "Why should I trust those strange people who work in artificial intelligence, wear the wrong clothes and have funny hairstyles. And look at the cars they drive. Not our kind of people!" The challenge in communities is to overcome these hurdles. You need trust but also tolerance and transparency to do that.

Trust in our community has three dimensions: trust that your partner is motivated to help you *(benevolence),* that your partner has the ability to help *(competence),* and that the partner will protect your valuable knowledge *(security)*.[6] In all three dimensions, trust can be created over greater distances thanks to the team transparency that has been made possible by new communication technologies. Philippe Mauchard, one of the founders of the professional artificial intelligence group McKinsey Solutions, puts it as follows: "Trust is the link that keeps the community together. Real relationships of trust are indispensable."

---

[6] Nussbaum (2004).

5 Foundations of the Successful Professional Community

Can Anybody Be Trusted Anymore?

Ok, I may be old-fashioned, but I notice that basic trust is slowly disappearing from our traditional professions. Who nowadays trusts his or her dentist to do the right things to his or her teeth and then send a fair invoice? Where is the trusted advisor for companies and entrepreneurs? Where is the accountant who checks my figures without overcharging me? And how is it possible that even the family solicitor now acts like a commercial lawyer? In a recent press interview, Dutch royal Prince Constantijn explained his success in leading the venture firm Techleap: "My strength is that I do not have an immediate personal gain in mind and always look at long-term success." Is he the only one left?

Trust arrives on foot and departs on horseback

The gradual waning of trust in the professions unfortunately reflects a societal development. "Trust is good, control is better," according to Lenin. It describes a growing way of thinking and behaving. We have less and less trust in our fellow human beings, become suspicious, and then check and check again. When conflict threatens, the first thing we do is call our lawyer, who more often than not thrives on legal conflicts. When clients display these attitudes, perhaps professionals adapt and lose some of their natural, trustworthy way of working. They are, after all, part of the same society that is apparently migrating to different values.

I'm sure it must have taken many years before this basic loss of trust in the professions became obvious. In many respects, we are all conservative and we dislike change. Unless change is really needed or wanted, we prefer the fundamental certainties of life, until…… Trust is also eminently practical in today's business world with its ever-increasing complexity of personal and professional life.

You cannot really question every service that you receive. We like to use terms such as trusted advisor and counselor, particularly when we are in a vulnerable business situation and need in-depth professional knowledge. Perhaps the medical doctor is the only person we still really trust. But we have no choice, do we?

You cannot avoid trust

The essential fact remains: one cannot enjoy a decent life without trust. Do you install webcams in and around your house to check on your partner? Do you hire detectives to follow your kids? Unfortunately, many of your subordinates' activities are beyond your control, and spying on them is apparently illegal in most countries. So, you have to trust them! Raising a family, leading people, receiving services in areas we do not understand ourselves—it is all about trust.

(continued)

> (continued)
>
> And, by the way, the cost of control is very high. Not only in terms of manpower, but also because of the demotivation that it entails. People cannot become excited about their work if they feel that they are continually being checked on. Most managers understand that it is far better to accept a minimum of theft in the store than to have cameras all over the place. It is interesting to note that the highest levels of quality often go together with low levels of control. Advanced software companies hold their programmers responsible and no longer have program testers. What about making sure you have the right culture in your organization?
>
> You cannot make profits with your company in this competitive world without a modicum of trust. Repression is too expensive.
>
> **Turning the tide for trust**
>
> Hopefully, I have made my point that it is very destructive for society if we can no longer trust high-level professionals who have a deep understanding of fields that we really need but do not master ourselves.
>
> Suggestions for dealing with this? "Be much more conscientious about the real value that you deliver to your client and communicate intensively about your performance" is one suggestion. Another is: "We need to be much more transparent and show how we operate." Sometimes, we become preoccupied with our project and profession, and lose our audience—i.e., our client—in the process. Our credibility in society is declining, as people no longer understand what the professional and his or her profession deliver. What is left are the complaints about our excessive fees, which is an unfortunate outcome.
>
> This is something we have to change. We as professionals must take the lead in this, start promoting a different position, and be proactive in gaining and earning the trust of society and clients. The abovementioned suggestions are a start. Just give them a try!

5.5.2 Tolerance

We see tolerance as the second most important quality for those who are working in a community context. Why would someone be more tolerant in a community than in a "normal" working environment? The perfect engagement for a community is a project in which several very different disciplines need to collaborate closely to achieve an optimal result. By definition, this means that the project participants have different backgrounds and that professional cooperation will probably be a challenge. Professionals/team members may rationally understand the value of their mixed team composition. But when actually doing the work, they will be struck by the differences in behavior and work styles, and in some cases, they might even feel that their classic rules of engagement are being violated.

This all means that the degree of acceptance between team members must be impressively high, which calls for a very tolerant mindset.

Professionals may experience irritation, because of obviously unprofessional behavior or concern about the quality of the work, which may lead to an inability to take responsibility for a result. This can escalate into frustration and anger when a colleague does not react appropriately to a perceived misstep in carrying out the work or into disbelief in the usefulness of the mixed team and, finally, into an unwillingness to adopt a learning mode. All these reactions can be regarded as normal and understandable. Therefore, community teams must learn to be tolerant and to ask questions instead of judging, to overstep their own emotions, look for the plusses, and learn to operate in a multidisciplinary team. What may help is an explicit team-building effort at the outset. For instance, a two-day working session, including a good night at the bar to dig deep in each other's minds and feelings, may do wonders. This team-building can of course be achieved in other ways, too!

Tolerance only for the real community champions?

5.5.3 Transparency

In a way, our third "soft factor" is a condition for effective trust and tolerance. After all, what is transparency all about? A sound contract may suffice in order to cooperate with parties you do not know well or with whom you mainly have a business connection. In a professional community, explicit work agreements between partners are necessary, but not enough. When a sudden assignment arises and the community must quickly come up with a winning proposal, there must be rapid understanding between members of what each of them can expect from the other. Explicit agreements and reports are not enough to ensure that they trust each other and perform well, but trust will exist when transparency becomes a key element of effective teamwork.[7] Do not hide what does not necessarily have to be hidden. Be open about how you act and the reasons for your actions. Many professionals are often overly cautious about sharing their professional knowledge, methods, and ways of operating. In many instances, there are no logical reasons for this. It is rare that a colleague has skills or know-how that needs to be hidden from other community members, especially when those fellow professionals are not in the same field. After all, the methods of one profession are useless to a specialist in another area, but sharing successful practices from outside the field is very useful in helping professionals to understand how colleagues work. Therefore, an open mind and a willingness to learn from each other will foster the functioning of the community. Transparency and openness in sharing will help members to trust each other and encourage them to be tolerant.

---

[7] Vlaar et al. (2007).

5 Foundations of the Successful Professional Community

Too much transparency can frighten you

The following is a real-life and very successful case about trust and cooperation in a professional firm:

> Eric, head of the chemical industry practice at an international consultancy, talks about cooperation between his specialist team, which he (a Frenchman) leads from London, and the local office of his firm in Amsterdam. "We work for every chemical company in the Netherlands of a certain size. (...) With our Dutch counterparts, we realized that we could not do without each other. I did not know the Dutch environment and did not have the time to find out more. Especially since my practice extends across Europe, not to mention the major assignments in the Middle East. I live in London, travel a lot and have little opportunity to indulge in philosophical conversations with my client company and its middle management. I leave that to my office manager in Amsterdam.

> That goes well until the next project has to be staffed. I think it makes sense for my practitioners to be deployed. The older consultants are desperately needed at the client company, because they know the industry and I want to give my youngsters experience. Moreover, this is of course good for my practice's turnover and margin. But my colleague—head of the Amsterdam office—naturally wants to give his own strategy and organization experts the opportunity. They also know the company culture, the socio-political environment and the local market best. In the first few years, we fought quite a lot about that. Then we agreed during a long dinner that we would only be able to come out of this if we both made our commitment so large

that we each had the feeling of having made 60% of the contribution and only having enjoyed 40% of the benefits. Occasionally we talk about it and ask each other: "Do you have the feeling again this time that you have done more than I did?" We trust each other. I am confident that my colleague will be fully committed to my practice in his marketing and account management programs and will involve me when he sells a new chemical project. For example, in organizational studies and other projects where knowledge of the Dutch language and culture are important. He, in turn, trusts that I will include a couple of his juniors in my exciting strategy projects and involve him when my client starts a new assignment at the end of the current project. At the end of the year, we see again and again that we could have gained more from the collaboration in the short term and that over the longer term, we have amazing success."

Eric's story about his cross-border cooperation offers a striking example of true collegiality in a community setting.

5.6 Growth: The Great Imperative

Growth in revenues and headcount appears to be a great ambition of most professional firms. They tend to keep tabs on how their revenues and headcount stack up against the competition. In contrast, some professionals believe that enough is enough and that they are quite comfortable with the size of their practice. Sensible arguments are that young generations appreciate the "slack" that an organization without growth may give to its staff. Seniors may feel comfortable with their firm as it is ("It will last out my career"). Nonetheless, there are important reasons to choose growth.

The intuitively easy reason is that growth enhances the prestige of the firm, although, admittedly, there are many very prestigious exceptions. The New York law firm of Wachtell, Lipton, Rosen & Katz, for example, has the highest earnings per professional in the business—more than $3mln for each lawyer—but no growth. For most of us, it simply sounds better to say "our staff grew by 20%" or "we made record revenues." These are signs of good health and business sustainability.

A second reason is dynamism. Experience shows that growing companies are structurally more profitable than stagnating or declining companies. One obvious reason is that fixed costs tend to lag the growth (or reduction) in revenues. Staff recruitment is usually somewhat behind and staff investments for example in training and supporting facilities are decidedly behind. As result, there is work pressure on existing staff and a risk that quality may suffer. At the same time, however, the margins are excellent. The opposite is of course true when revenues go down, which explains why it is so difficult to maintain profitability in a declining business. But the most important argument for growth is the "breathing space" that it generates for new people and new ideas to develop. If we take a small specialized law firm with five partners as a simple example: without growth, the bright, young new generation of lawyers will on average have to work and wait in training mode for twenty years or more before one of the partner spots becomes available.

Many ambitious associates may feel after five or six years that they are ready for partnership. Bad luck, however, as no space is available. In a growing environment, it should be no problem to promote a junior to partnership as soon as he is qualified.

Growth in a stable marketplace without innovation is difficult. Innovating with a team versed in legacy skills is difficult. The community provides the firm with links that enable innovation and growth. Growth motivates and creates new opportunities to build synergies. Building a professional service community becomes doable and even easy when the vision and mission are growth-oriented. Without growth, the path becomes very rocky.

5.7 Synergy: Translating Strong Foundations into Measurable Success

We now have a well-designed business model and the foundations of our community are all in order. The next step will be for us to observe the synergies that cause the value of our community to exceed that of its members. After all, the word synergy derives from the Greek συνεργία (synergia) and stands for the creation of a whole that is greater than the simple sum of its parts. Synergies are measurable indicators that we have made the right moves in setting up our structure and foundations, even before we observe an increase in bottom-line growth and margins. Our synergy potential is greatest in a number of community functions, including:

- Knowledge sharing thanks to the connectivity of our systems and databases, and good relations between community members.
- The success of a common community brand/reputation that supports marketing, sales, and delivery by the individual members.
- Service development and delivery in which community members join forces in delivery and in innovating new services.
- Client management in which members work together to acquire target clients and maintain relations with existing clients.
- The execution of complex projects that require a variety of skills and a wide range of expertise.

In a number of other areas, such as skills and organization, a lot can be gained from sharing resources and experience. And resource sharing is of

5 Foundations of the Successful Professional Community

Function	Potential	Comments
Vision/Strategy		Community vision may require compromise from the members
Brainpower		Exchange of manpower to meet excess/deficit in demand
Skills/Competencies		Learning potential from partners
Knowledge		Share information, knowledge, insight
Culture		Learning potential from partners
Organization		Sharing of staff functions (marketing, training, etc)
Economics		Stronger financial base for risk-sharing
Brand/Reputation		Stronger shared brand
Services		Joint offerings with more breadth and depth
Clients		More resources to meet client needs

Fig. 5.1 Synergy potential of communities

course important in the area of economics, particularly since client demand for more risk-sharing is gradually increasing.

The impact of synergy is more indirect but no less important in areas such as vision, strategy, and culture, where the effects of alignment will be felt strongly, but later.

The following table summarizes the main areas of synergy potential (see Fig. 5.1).

5.8 Innovation and Renewal

5.8.1 Why Innovate?

When the community has been set up properly and is working well, it presumably enters a period of bliss: happy clients and staff, solid workload, and healthy economics. But this is deceptive. The world actually sees regular arrivals of black swans, as the Lehman and COVID-19 crises have shown. Sooner or later, our professional services will again be disrupted in ways we cannot foresee. Professional service providers can prepare for these threats in a couple of ways. The first option is for firms to wait until there is disruption and then trust in their flexibility, for example, in restructuring their member portfolio. Another, more exciting option is to innovate and meet the challenges with new services and a new approach. That is where innovation comes in. According to the former strategy guru Clayton Christensen of Harvard, pioneering innovation is the key to the company's future success.[8] We will have to innovate to ensure the future of our office.[9]

Innovation means thinking about new services, about putting new value propositions on the market, whether or not in combination with a different revenue model. And it includes interacting with the client in new ways, for example by working with mixed teams or including contracts that carry risk. The delivery process can be redesigned, often with much use of ICT. This has consequences for the skills required and the organization, but also for the organization of the firm and even its financial structure—needed to support more risky client relations.

Innovation requires entrepreneurship, flexibility, a desire to explore, and a willingness to run the associated operational risks. People will also have to be willing to give up existing ways of working: innovation always comes after creative destruction.[10] We must realize, however, that the success rate of innovation projects is generally not very high.

---

[8] Christensen et al. (2015).
[9] Anand et al. (2007).
[10] Kvålshaugen et al. (2015).

5 Foundations of the Successful Professional Community

It's dogged that does it

Depending on the way it is calculated, between 10 and at most 30 percent of innovation initiatives that are launched ultimately succeed. This means that many professionals who enthusiastically embark on a project will have to cope with eventual disappointment. In the vast majority of cases, this cannot be blamed on their lack of talent and motivation. The business proposition was simply wrong or untimely. Or it was a case of bad luck: a promising client who decided at the last minute to postpone for a year, or the essential expert who was lured away to another job. Successful entrepreneurship requires patience and perseverance. And understanding from the organization when the failed innovator returns to the fold. But most traditional professional firms have little experience with innovation and little patience. How, then, should the firm deal with innovation? To achieve a successful innovation stream, windows should be opened and new ways explored.[11]

Fortunately, the professional community provides a perfect environment for innovation. New, younger participants who come up with new ideas can set up their own business within the community, while the established units continue their successful work. Thanks to the freedom they have in the community, they can develop their own business model, experiment, and explore. The established firms can benefit from the new services and see how well the business model of newcomers works, without being threatened in their own identity. Research has shown that

---

[11] Fu et al. (2016), Senge et al. (1994).

centralization has a negative impact on innovation.[12] This explains why large firms such as PWC and McKinsey invest in independent subsidiaries. And we notice that the real breakthroughs, such as the AI-supported legal profession, come from startups.

5.8.2 Alienation and Spin-Offs Threaten

However, innovation still requires nurturing in the community. Alienation and spin-off of an innovative project constantly threaten. If the innovation team and the existing community fail to appreciate each other's values and culture, they will not be able to benefit. If, for example, the community partners try to maximize the income of their seniors while the innovation team asks for resources to develop technology and grow, it will be difficult to combine the two. Innovation must still fit in with the existing work of the community's participants and the values and culture of the new team cannot conflict with what existing participants stand for.

5.8.3 How Do we Strengthen Innovation and Keep Innovative Teams on Board?

If a community is to have a successful series of innovations, it must be extroverted and have a good team, with sufficient initiative delegated to

---

[12] Perra et al. (2017).

lower levels. Concerning outward orientation: an innovation only makes sense if it meets the current or future needs of the client. The leadership must bridge the values and culture of the various participants so that they appreciate each other and work together. To be able to develop synergies, the traditional and innovative participants will have to share ideas and needs for innovation. This synergy comes from mutual understanding and the motivation to collaborate. Both are highly dependent on effective communication. A good team spirit helps enormously. This can be strengthened by organizing joint training sessions and by rotating team members between the participating firms.[13]

5.8.4 How Do we Start and Manage Innovation?

The question remains how the leadership of the community should handle innovation. If an innovation initiative fits in with an existing activity in the community, it seems a good idea to further develop that innovation in one of the existing offices. The same applies if there is a strong affinity with the values and culture of the existing participants. If, however, the connection with existing processes and/or values is weak, then a spin-off within the community must be considered. In that sense, the community shows its unique ability to maintain links between otherwise independent units. No other business model provides that freedom.

---

[13] Semadeni and Anderson (2010).

References

Anand, N., Gardner, H. K., & Morris, T. (2007). Knowledge-based innovation: Emergence and embedding of new practice areas in management consulting firms. *Academy of Management Journal, 50*(2), 406–428.

Blomgren, M., & Waks, C. (2015). Coping with contradictions: Hybrid professionals managing institutional complexity. *Journal of Professions and Organization, 2*(1), 78–102.

Christensen, C. M., Raynor, M., & McDonald, R. (2015). What is disruptive innovation. *Harvard Business Review, 93*(12), 44–53.

Faulconbridge, J., & Muzio, D. (2008). Re-inserting the professional in the study of PSFs. *Global Networks, 7*(3), 249–270.

Fu, N., Flood, P., & Morris, T. (2016). Organizational ambidexterity and professional firm performance: The role of organizational capital. *Journal of Professions and Organization, 3*(1), 1–16.

Gluckler, J., & Armbruster, T. (2003). Bridging uncertainty in management consulting: The mechanisms of trust and networked reputation. *Organization Studies, 24*, 269–297.

Heckscher, C., & Adler, P. S. (2006). *The firm as collaborative community: Reconstructing Trust in the Knowledge Economy.* Oxford University Press.

Ibarra, H., & Obodaru, O. (2016). Betwixt and between identities: Liminal experience in contemporary careers. *Research in Organizational Behaviour, 36*, 47–64.

Kvålshaugen, R., Hydle, K. M., & Brehmer, P. O. (2015). Innovative capabilities in international professional service firms: Enabling trade-offs between past, present, and future service provision. *Journal of Professions and Organization, 2*(2), 148–167.

Lorsch, J. W., & Tierney, T. J. (2002). *Aligning the stars: How to succeed when professionals drive results.* Harvard Business School Press.

Nussbaum, H. (2004). Will security enhance trust online? In N. M. Ashkanasy et al. (Eds.), *Trust and distrust in organizations. Dilemmas and approaches* (pp. 164–178). Sage Publishing.

Perra, D. B., Sidhu, J. S., & Volberda, H. W. (2017). How Do Established Firms Produce Breakthrough Innovations? Managerial Identity-Dissemination Discourse and The Creation of Novel Product-Market Solutions. *Journal of Product Innovation Management, 34*(4), 509–525.

Semadeni, M., & Anderson, B. S. (2010). The follower's dilemma: Innovation and imitation in the professional services industry. *Academy of Management Journal, 53*(5), 1175–1193.

Senge, P. M., Kleiner, A., Roberts, C., Ross, R. B., & Smith, B. J. (1994). *The fifth discipline Fieldbook. Strategies and tools for building a learning organisation.* Doubleday.

Vlaar, P. W. L., Van den Bosch, F. A. J., & Volberda, H. W. (2007). On the Evolution of Trust, Distrust, and Formal Coordination and Control in Interorganizational Relationships: Toward an Integrative Framework. *Group & Organization Management, 32*(4), 407–429.

6

Fieldwork: Monday Morning Actions

6.1 Off to Work!

We hope you found the preceding chapters informative and inspiring. But the proof of success is in the action: it is Monday morning and we must act now so as not to risk losing another week. So, here we go. We understand why our old archetypes are no longer the best way to organize our professional services, if only due to the disruptions of technology, the pressing demands of our new generation of staff members and critical clients, and because of our increasing ineffectiveness in applying our super-specializations in the increasingly complex business of our clients. We have discussed the professional business model and seen what has to change in each of its key functions. And we have seen the professional community as the answer for many of us. What do we do?

Our action schedule is divided into four steps: an orientation step (1) in which we identify the disruptions and take a hard-nosed look at our current way of doing business. This leads to step (2) in which we take a closer look at our business model and determine what needs to be changed. At this point we also invite our preferred partners to join in the discussion. Step (3) is dedicated to constructing our professional community. In step (4) we start working toward success while checking whether all the foundations are in place. In the meanwhile, we need to make sure that the colleagues in our own and our partners' firms continue to support our new approach.

6.2 Understand Our Current Strategic Position and Disruptions

6.2.1 Step 1: Follows Chapter 1 of This Book

This is an informative step in which we gather external inputs, adding our own people's ideas as we proceed. This means interviews with clients and prospective clients, staff, and prospective staff. And with own experts and juniors. And, where needed, external experts, for example to learn more about current and future competition.

Some of the Questions That We Should Ask in This Step

- How do our clients perceive our services? Are they still completely satisfied, or are they inviting new competitors? Are their demands changing—different services, different ways of working together, new technologies, different payment methods?
- Are we still attracting the kind of juniors that we need? And are we able to retain them? What do they want that we cannot provide? And where are they going?
- Are we encountering new competition? From small, low-cost boutiques, from technology-based firms, from large multiservice firms, or from in-house staff departments? What does our "nightmare" competitor look like?
- Are we making the best use of new technologies, adopting them in our existing organization and looking for new ways to gain access? Or are we ignoring them and leaving that arena to newcomers?
- What is our "burning platform" for change? Is there a clearly urgent need that will help us to overcome the hurdles and resistance to change that we can expect?

6.3 Evaluate Our Business Model

6.3.1 Step 2: Follows Chapters 2 and 3 of This Book

The objective of this step is to pinpoint where our biggest problems and challenges lie, and find out how these are connected with the existing business model. In this step, it will also be valuable to develop a vision of our business 5–10 years from now. This vision typically includes an outline of the services that we would like to supply, the clients we like to serve, the type of people working for us, and the competitors that we face. This is typically a job for current and potential leaders of our new business. Questions we should ask ourselves include:

- What will our business model and its 10 functions described in Chap. 2 look like and how will it meet the disruptive challenges of the future?
- Which examples from competitors and other suppliers would we like to use in redefining our business model? What can we learn from the case examples of Chap. 3?

Assemble the community model...

6.4 Assemble Our Community Model

6.4.1 Step 3: Follows Chapter 4 of This Book

Once the starting members of the community have been identified, we can set up a constituting group of seniors who can kick off the discussion about the common vision and form of the community. This debate requires careful preparation, since the arguments have to be supported by facts wherever possible.

6.4.2 Agree on a Vision for the Community and Its Core Consequences: Reputation, Brand, Standards

When discussing our vision, the main questions relate to:

- The common vision and mission that our community should have, the common services to start with, and to which preferred clients.
- The main principles that will drive the design of our community. Which of the 10 functions do we want to share, and where do we want to maintain independence?
- Which reputation and brand do we want to establish with our existing and future clients, staff, and other stakeholders. And which attributes are vital and which are important or relevant?
- How can we position the community in such a way that the members' brand and reputation are strengthened by the community?
- What are our quality standards and how do we make sure that these are maintained?

6.4.3 Decide on the Leadership of Our Community and Its Pop-Up Projects

At this point, we should decide which leadership positions are needed and who will fill them, at least during the startup phase. The same applies to the rules for the pop-up teams that sell and perform projects, and the designation of team leaders to develop accounts and perform the work. We should also appoint people to supervise the leadership and determine their powers.

6.4.4 Define Our Sources of Professional Value: Brainpower, Competences, Knowledge

At this stage, it becomes advisable to appoint task forces to develop policy, development needs, and actions for each relevant area.

Questions we should ask ourselves include:

- Can/should the community support recruitment by its members? If so, how? Does the community change the recruitment profile of its members?
- What are the skills and knowledge gaps in our community? How can we best share skills and knowledge between community members?
- What kind of ICT/database infrastructure is needed to enable the sharing of staff, skills, and knowledge? Who should we recruit to manage central ICT and recruitment?

6.4.5 Determine Our Organization, Economics, Culture, Strategy

We now have to create designs for the organization and each of its functions. These will include a centralized dimension, with or without dedicated manpower, and a main body of responsibilities that is carried out by member organizations of the community. Secondly, a leadership, together with control and supervisory responsibilities, will have to be appointed for each of the community's main functions.

These tasks require considerable compromise and will be a first test of the strength of the community and its vision. Questions we should ask ourselves include:

- How should we structure the community to have power where needed and subsidiarity for the rest?
- Which processes should cover the key community functions, such as marketing, sales, recruitment, training, account management, branding, and quality control?
- How can we ensure that members will support community functions, and how will the community enforce its policy rulings among its members?
- How will community functions be funded?

6.5 Invite Partners to Our Professional Community

6.5.1 Make Sure the Foundations of Our Professional Service Community Are in Place: Step 4: Following Chapter 5 of This Book

In this step, we establish our community. This requires a careful initial selection of the partners to be invited. Partners who fill the gaps in the capabilities that we will need in order to meet the disruptions that we face. Partners who can contribute skills, knowledge, creativity, or a network of attractive clients. Partners with staff, financing, and other resources. Partners who can innovate. But these partners also have to be compatible in terms of their vision, mission, and core values.

6.5.2 Get Our Colleagues On board

It may well be that our colleagues are not all swept away by the concept of a professional community. Or we just know how our colleagues are feeling about any innovation or change in the existing business model of our firm: "so far, so good" and "why to change something that is doing well," concluding with "what, me worry?" Not everybody will be excited by the prospect of first going through a logic and rational process of designing an appropriate community model for our firm and then changing their work habits rather thoroughly to make it work: Those who are busy with change all the time in their client assignments end up being scared to death for changes in their own firm. The saying goes "the children of the doctor are always sick," but unfortunately, the doctors have no time to worry! The following are some of the questions that a critic or non-believers can ask and a few suggestions on how to get the alignment and motivation up.

"We do not fully understand how our community will work".

Invite a speaker who works in multidisciplinary communities. For instance from advertising or from the artistic fields (movies, stage performances), the construction industry, or aerospace. The point is to show that cooperation on one project by many very different professions is possible, useful, and often required. And that it adds a lot to the result. Or invite a speaker from the same profession (or one of the authors of this book) who already has experience in working in a community.

A different approach would involve presenting an overview of the forces that will disrupt our firm and the effects on a shorter and longer timeframe. Then show and discuss the limits of incremental improvement actions. The community model can then be introduced as a general way to achieve sustainability in the future. We don't have to make it complicated. Just one case may do the trick. The idea is that it can convince the distractors that it is all not very difficult and in fact quite doable.

6 Fieldwork: Monday Morning Actions

"Is our community going to be viable?"

A good idea is to select and execute a suitable client assignment that can be handled by engaging different disciplines and professions from a community. This may mean that we must select partners from different professions which are new to us. This will make the point and demonstrates how the concept works in your own environment. Alternatively, it may be a good idea to select and discuss several successful cases from our professional field and present them as evidence (authors may help). A third option is to design (perhaps with some outside help) a simulation of a functioning community.

"Who are going to be the champions for change?"

Leverage young and ambitious energy: NewGen is one of the driving forces for change toward the professional community. The idea is to engage those in building up the community and convince the older generations. A group must be formed consisting of the "bright and young," who are willing to lead the development. They are the front troopers, not only designing but also acting in reality including concrete client assignments. If successful, the whole firm will follow.

What Is our Plan for Moving Ahead?

Somewhat surprisingly, professional firms are often weak in designing and deciding their own strategy. The realization of the extent and seriousness of the disruption should be the trigger to start up a serious effort to come to a new (or even a) strategy of the firm. Then one only has to be sure that the business model is also part of this study and strategy and that the concept of a community will be part of the options. The outcome may automatically lead toward a professional community.

6.6 Make Sure We Remain on Track

We have now started working as a community and the time has come to check whether we are strong enough to continue and to take away the last impediments to our effective operation. This is the job of the community leadership, supported by seniors of a few critical member organizations. It may also involve real investments and real influencing leverage, for example when we look at the interconnection of information systems or the imposition of commonality in branding and quality standards. We should ask the following questions when we consider the three "C"s. Are our vision and brand strong enough to support the connection and alignment of the key community functions? Are the members' knowledge systems effectively connected? Are formal/informal controls in place for quality and branding? Have we selected the right partners with a group of professionals that will deliver? We can then look at the three "T"s and ask: do we have sufficient trust, transparency, and tolerance? Is this a sound enough basis for real synergies and innovation?

All these questions lead to the next point: if one of these foundations is found wanting, how can and should we correct it? Once we have made sure the foundations are in good shape, we can be confident that our professional community has started on a path to success.

Closing Remarks

It is our firm belief that professions and professionals will change due to a number of disruptive forces. We mentioned four categories: technology, new generations, critical clients, and complexity. It is hard to predict which of them will be more disruptive than the others. This will also vary in each profession and individual firm. But change is inevitable! And the strategy for coping with disruptive change will lie in a form of community modeling. We are convinced in particular that the assignments that clients will give us will change in nature. The pure, deeply specialist professional and firm will not disappear, but an increasing number of assignments will be oriented toward a broader, more holistic approach involving many competences, while at the same time the emphasis is on rapid implementation of the recommendations.

As we have seen in the first chapters of this book, small is beautiful. A firm without too many professionals and that has a good focus suits the new generations best. If this firm is then embedded in a flexible professional community, all the conditions are in place for the members to grow and flourish as professionals. That is the world you should work toward.

Our ideas becoming reality depends to a large extent on the willingness of seniors to develop and change. With a mentality of "après moi le déluge," most established firms will not make the right moves. And in a hypercompetitive world, this means that their sandwich will be eaten by new firms popping up with new ideas and the right energy and drive to quickly conquer the market. So, be the first to move and don't be afraid to fail. And our best advice to conclude is: talk about these changes with your best clients.

By the time you read this, we assume that you will have started working with a few trusted member firms in a community with great promise. You will doubtless run into challenges. After all, you are embarking on an ocean voyage with a set of crew members who all have their own journeys behind them. At sea, the weather changes; the complexity and dynamics of this world are increasing. Your crew members may change and some may be end up being replaced. But as long as you keep your eye on your compass—your mission—and make sure that the seven foundations remain strong and the business model works—you will make it.

After All

It ought to be remembered that there is nothing more difficult to undertake, more perilous to conduct, or more uncertain in its success, than to taking the lead in the introduction of a new order of things (*Niccoló Machiavelli,* the Prince).

Afterthoughts

The New Professional Service Firm provides a solution for those who are caught between the archetypes of their past and the disruptive challenges of the future. Written by three knowledgeable authors who together have more than 100 years' experience in strategy and organization. One very knowledgeable consultant with a focus on analysis and design, a critical and demanding professor with a background in strategy and innovation, and another experienced consultant with a passion for people management and cultural change: our diverse backgrounds gave us a lot of synergy!

We benefited immensely from the advice provided by our professional friends and former colleagues, too many to list. But we do want to mention those who helped us develop the case descriptions that are a foundation of this book: David Teece of BRG—the Berkeley Research Group, Liann Eden and Marion Wanders of Eden McCallum, Charley Moore of Rocket Lawyer, Malcolm Ross of Merlin, Henk Cohen of BSO, Laurie Rowan and Erin Giglia of the Montage Group, and Jerold Savin of CTCG.

158 Afterthoughts

And in the closing remarks time has come for the authors to express their gratitude for an archetype that combines support, patience, a hearing ear, and critical eye as well as strategic guidance, in the form of our respective partnerships with and Klaske, Anna, and Elena.

Index

A
Aberkyn, 11
Accenture, 11, 50
Accountability, 19
Account coordinator, 91, 112, 124
Account leader, 87
Account management, 10, 53, 67, 68, 80, 88, 98, 99, 134, 150
Alfa Accountants and Advisors, 16
Alignment, 52, 68, 104, 137, 152
AlixPartners, 9
Allen & Overy, 6, 7
Alvarez & Marsal, 9
Amazon, 74
Ambiguity, 58
Archetype, 47, 55, 58, 59, 85, 89, 90, 123, 145, 157, 158
Arthur Andersen, 2
Artificial intelligence (AI), 3, 11, 13, 17, 38, 42, 54, 59, 73, 128
Arthur D. Little, 26
ASI, xvi
Auction Technologies, 68
Audit, 3, 4, 14, 20, 26, 54, 108
Axiom, 53

B
Bain, 10, 68
Baker McKenzie, 6, 50
BCG, 50, 60, 68
Berenschot, 10
Berkeley Research Group (BRG), 65, 66, 70, 77–82
Berkeley University, 78
Best friends, 54, 60, 66
Big data, 13, 59, 69, 73
Booz & Company, xvii, 2, 107
Brainpower, 88, 89, 92–97, 108, 120, 149, 150
Brand, 149, 154
Braxton, 2, 10, 106

Bredin Prat, 54
Bureau for Software Development (BSO), 65, 75, 76, 82
Business model, xiv, 2, 7, 12, 30, 45, 47, 49, 59, 61, 81, 85–89, 95, 106, 108, 117, 120, 123, 136, 139, 141, 145, 147, 148, 152, 154, 156

C
Cambridge Technology Consulting Group (CTCG), 66, 67
Christenson, 138
Coaching, 16, 20, 49, 54, 66, 68, 93, 123
Complexity, 14, 25, 26, 40, 49, 55, 99, 108, 129, 155, 156
Connection, 2, 17, 37, 40, 50, 95, 117, 123, 132, 141, 154
Connectivity, 97, 119, 120, 136
Control, 52, 72, 75, 76, 81, 82, 87, 88, 90, 98, 121, 123, 127, 129, 130, 150, 154
COVID-19, 13, 22, 72
Creativity, 37, 39, 60, 88, 93, 151
Culture, 39, 46, 48, 55, 58, 68, 76, 81, 82, 86, 98–100, 102, 112, 121, 123, 130, 133, 134, 137, 140, 141, 150

D
Debevoise & Plimpton, 2
De Brauw, 54
Deloitte, 6, 11, 14, 15, 25, 50
Dentons, 6
Deutsche Telekom, 68

Digital-McKinsey, 11
Dynamic capability, 95

E
Economics, 89, 98–99, 137, 150
Eden McCallum, 53, 66, 68–70, 82
Eggsplore, 11
Expertise, xiii, 2, 10, 11, 14, 37, 39, 42, 49, 50, 67, 70, 79, 82, 108, 136
Exploitation, 58
Exploration, 58, 59
EY, 11, 50, 111

F
Financing, 97, 151
Flexfirm, 53–56, 58, 85, 88, 89
Flexibility, 7, 19, 29, 58, 61, 70, 81, 82, 88–90, 94, 102, 103, 138

G
Galan, xvi
Gentlemen's club, 47, 49, 55, 56, 85, 89, 94, 106, 118
Giglia, 70
Goldman Sachs, 25
Google, 74
Growth, 117, 134, 135

H
Harvard, 138
Headcount, 134
Hengeler Mueller, 54
Horwath, 9

I

InterLaw, 54
Investments, 44, 49, 50, 54–57, 69, 72, 76, 77, 121, 123, 135, 154

J

Jan Hommen, 19

K

Key account, 81, 91
Kienhuis Hoving, 8
Knowledge, 119, 120, 127–129, 132, 134, 136, 150
KPMG, 19, 26, 50

L

Leadership, 86, 87, 89–92, 98–102, 111, 112, 121, 141
LeanLawyer, 53
Legal department, 24, 72
Lehman, 9, 137
Lex Machina, 14–15
Lex Mundi, 54
Lloyd Blankfein, 25
LUNAR, 11
Lünendonk & Hossenfelder, 9

M

Machiavelli, 156
Magic Circle, 7
Malcolm Ross, 68
Management, 89, 90, 94, 97–99, 101, 103, 104, 108, 110, 112, 123, 133, 136, 157
Marketing, 91, 101, 102, 110, 112, 114, 121, 123, 134, 136

McKinsey, 9, 10, 39, 43, 50, 68, 140
McKinsey Analytics, 11
McKinsey Implementation Services, 11
McKinsey Solutions, 11, 59, 123, 128
McKinsey Transformation Services, 11
Merlin, 60, 65, 66, 68, 81, 82
Monitor, 10, 11, 68
Montage Group, 66, 70
Moore, 74
Motivation, 52, 68, 76, 94, 139, 141

N

Network, 4, 11, 29, 40, 50, 52, 55, 56, 60, 65, 68, 85, 88, 91, 98, 112, 113
NewGen, 4, 49, 54, 93
NPS Lab, 9
Nyenrode University, 18

O

Omnius, 53
Ooa, xvi
Organization, 147, 150, 154, 157
Origin, 76

P

Philips, 10, 19, 75, 76
Pop-up team, 90–92, 101, 112, 123, 149
Project leadership, 91
Project management, 17, 87, 88, 101
Public data, 96
PWC, 2, 6, 11, 50, 107, 140

Q

QuantumBlack, 11

R

RAND, xv
Rebel Group, 44
Recruitment, 4, 9, 20, 48, 55, 69, 72, 123, 135, 150
Relx Group, 15
Reputation, 7, 41, 46, 56, 67, 69, 71, 72, 86, 89, 90, 98, 104–107, 113, 118, 136, 149
Revenues, 10, 42, 58, 99, 109, 119, 121, 138
Robin Hood, 58
Rocket Lawyer, 66, 73, 82
Roland Berger, 16
Rowan, 70
Rules, 86, 88, 90, 97, 99, 101, 102, 104, 123, 126, 131, 149

S

SAP, 27
Savin, 66
Security, 97, 128
6 Sigma, 27
Simmons & Simmons, 7
Skills, 11, 13, 16, 29, 40, 46, 49, 55, 68, 78, 86, 89, 90, 92–97, 101, 108, 120, 125, 132, 135, 136, 138, 150, 151
Slaughter & May, 54, 60
Software, 2, 3, 14, 30, 31, 58, 61, 65–67, 73–76, 81, 119, 130
Spark Optimus, 39
Specialization, 26, 27, 31, 40, 97, 145
&Strategy, 107

Strategy, 9, 10, 16, 25, 42, 46, 59, 68, 69, 74, 78, 87–89, 99, 107, 113, 133, 134, 137, 138, 151, 153, 155, 157
Subsidiarity, 87, 88, 102, 140, 150
Sustainable Development Goals, 20
Synergy, 88, 157

T

Technology, 3, 14, 15, 26, 38, 65, 66, 68, 81, 82, 119, 123, 128, 140, 145, 147, 155
Teece, 77, 81
Tesco, 15
Thomas Lünendonk, 9
Transparency, 117, 126, 128, 132, 154
Trust, 154

U

Uría Menéndez, 54
USG, 53

V

VLT Labs, 11
Vodafone, 68
Volberda, xv

W

Wachtell Lipton Rosen & Katz, 7
WagenaarHoes, xvi
Wanders, 53, 69
Wintzen, 75
Work–life balance, 18, 20
World Law Group, 54
WPP, 121

GPSR Compliance
The European Union's (EU) General Product Safety Regulation (GPSR) is a set of rules that requires consumer products to be safe and our obligations to ensure this.

If you have any concerns about our products, you can contact us on

ProductSafety@springernature.com

In case Publisher is established outside the EU, the EU authorized representative is:

Springer Nature Customer Service Center GmbH
Europaplatz 3
69115 Heidelberg, Germany

www.ingramcontent.com/pod-product-compliance
Ingram Content Group UK Ltd.
Pitfield, Milton Keynes, MK11 3LW, UK
UKHW021249180426
11946UKWH00003B/33